DEV
CO
UN

Emily Kerr

Joshua Perry

illustrations by
Katherine Hardy

EAST DEVON

NORTH DEVON

SOUTH DEVON

CENTRAL CORNWALL

WEST CORNWALL

TOP FIVES

NOTES

This book belongs to:

EAST DEVON

NORTH DEVON

SOUTH DEVON

CENTRAL CORNWALL

WEST CORNWALL

TOP FIVES

TIN MINE

CONTENTS

EAST DEVON

NORTH DEVON

SOUTH DEVON

CENTRAL CORNWALL

WEST CORNWALL

TOP FIVES

MAP OF DEVON & CORNWALL

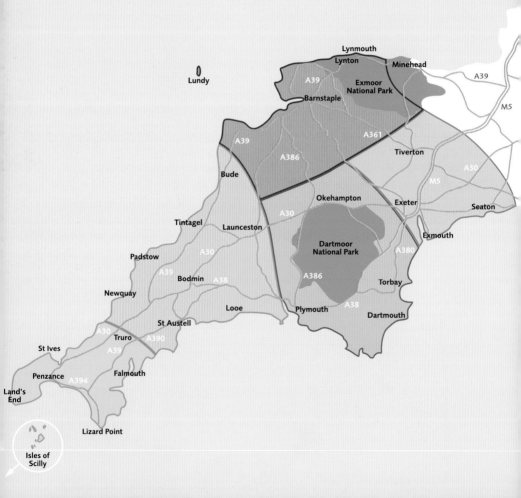

EAST DEVON

NORTH DEVON

SOUTH DEVON

CENTRAL CORNWALL

WEST CORNWALL

TOP FIVES

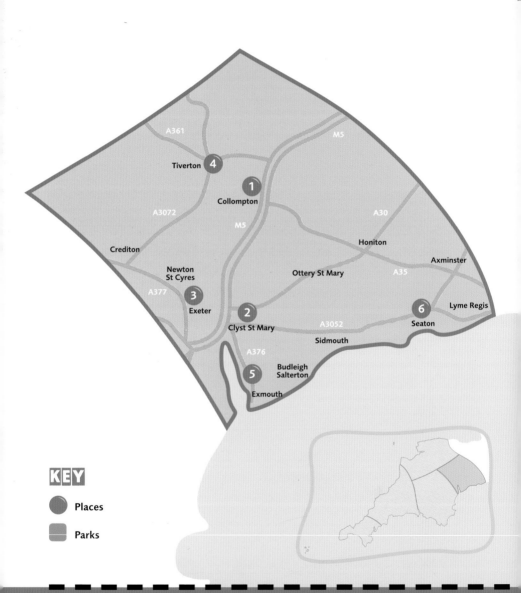

KEY

● Places

▬ Parks

EAST DEVON

NORTH DEVON

SOUTH DEVON

CENTRAL CORNWALL

WEST CORNWALL

TOP FIVES

BELOW EXETER

EXETER

DRIVE A DIGGER

...at Diggerland

Normally we wouldn't recommend driving a digger. They're too slow for the school run, and you might accidentally dig up half of the road. However, at Diggerland you'll definitely want to get behind the wheel!

Diggerland lets you drive and use real diggers. And there's much more to do than just shovelling mud - you can use diggers to find buried treasure, knock down skittles or dig a giant hole. You'll also get a chance to ride pedal-powered diggers, and even ride in a digger's shovel!

If you get bored of diggers (and we can't imagine that you will) there's also a Land Rover Safari, a soft-play centre, an adventure playground and dodgems to pass the time. We really *dig* this place!

Sticker Scores

5	4	3
DESTRUCTIVE DIGGER	SERIOUS SPADE	TERRIBLE TROWEL

2	1
SMALL SPOON	BARE HANDS

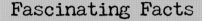

Make A Day Of It

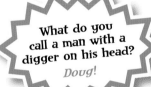 If moving machines are your thing, visit nearby Quad World, where you can drive a quad bike. Full protective clothing and tuition are provided.
www.quadworld.co.uk

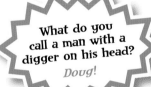 Crealy Great Adventure Park (see p12) is a theme park with water rides, roller coasters, log flumes, pirate ships and indoor play areas with slides and aerial walkways.
www.crealy.co.uk

What do you call a man with a digger on his head?
Doug!

← "Who's the man in the hat, Mum?"

Fascinating Facts

★ The inventor of JCBs (a man called Joe Cyril Bamford) was so confident in the strength of his machines that he created a display team of dancing diggers! These acrobatic machines raise themselves up on their digging arm in all kinds of curious ways. The Dancing Diggers still tour agricultural shows today.

★ Mirny Diamond Mine in Russia is the site of one of the biggest man-made holes in the world. It's 525 metres deep and almost a mile across. In fact it's so large that helicopters aren't allowed to fly over it because it has its own weather system which could suck them down!

PLAN YOUR VISIT ①

Diggerland

Verbeer Manor, Willand, Cullompton, EX15 2PE
www.diggerland.com

☎ 0871 227 7007

🕐 **Daily (peak) 10.00-17.00**
Opening hours vary out of season

£££

I want to go here ☐

EXPLORE AN ADVENTURE PARK

...at Crealy

Devon is full of places where you can have fun, but there's only one place where you can have a *crealy* good time!

Crealy is an awesome adventure park that's packed with rides, slides and more besides. Zip over to the action realm for race karts, dinosaur rides and bumper boats. Or, if it's raining, hang out in the adventure zone where you'll find giant drop slides, aerial walkways and climbing nets.

We particularly like the animals at Crealy. You can ride a pony, feed a goat, or be freaked out by creepy-crawlies. And if you stay on Crealy's campsite you'll be assigned your very own miniature pony for the whole of your visit!

Sticker Scores

5 ROLLER COASTER

4 LOG FLUME

3 DROP SLIDE

2 ROPE BRIDGE

1 DRINKS COASTER

Best Of The Rest

🔑 Make a splash on the Vortex water coaster. You sit on a dinghy and whizz down one of three different slides. Choose the middle one for the biggest drop!

🔑 Bash into boats on the Bumper Boats attraction. It's like dodgems on water . . . with added spray guns!

Top Tip

If you live in the area, ask Crealy's staff about how to join their Child Board of Directors. The theme park has a group of kid advisors who help them improve the park.

← Splash-tastic!

Similar Spots

🔑 Woodlands in Devon (see p125) has fantastic playgrounds as well as a zoo, animal petting and a bird of prey centre.
www.woodlandspark.com

🔑 Watermouth Castle is a smaller theme park near Ilfracombe with a wicked water park.
www.watermouthcastle.com

🔑 Flambards near Helston is another ace amusement park. We like the Canyon River Log Flume!
www.flambards.co.uk

🔑 There is also a Cornwall Crealy near Wadebridge.
www.crealy.co.uk/cornwall

PLAN YOUR VISIT ②

Crealy Great Adventure Park
Sidmouth Road, Exeter, EX5 1DR
www.crealy.co.uk/devon

📞 **01395 233 200**
🕐 **Daily (peak) 10.00-18.00**
   Opening hours vary throughout year

£££

I want to go here ☐

WALK UNDER EXETER

...through Exeter's Underground Passages

Unless you like strolling through sewers, the normal way to walk through a place is above ground. But in Exeter, you can explore beneath the city's streets!

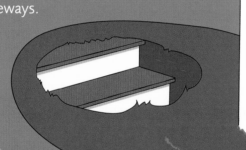

From above, Exeter looks like a normal university city. But look below and you'll find an underground network of tunnels built hundreds of years ago! Don a hard hat and follow your guide through the vaulted passageways. They used to contain pipes bringing fresh water from springs outside Exeter into the city.

Sticker Scores

5 TERRIFIC TUNNEL

4 PERFECT PASSAGE

3 WONDERFUL WALKWAY

2 STANDARD SHAFT

1 CAVED IN!

Look out for the awesome annual events. There's an Easter egg hunt and Halloween Gory Story tours every year, which turn a terrific tour into an *egg*-stravaganza or a *fright*-fully fun day out!

Make A Day Of It

🔑 See the highest waterfall in England. Canonteign Falls is also home to a children's assault course, a separate play area and a place to picnic. www.canonteignfalls.co.uk

🔑 Spot sculptures on the Exeter University Sculpture Trail. It includes one by Barbara Hepworth (see p106). www.exeter.ac.uk/sculpture

🔑 Make your own art at Make Art! It's a bit like pottery painting but with more choice of what to create. You can choose from jewellery, collages, paintings or ceramics. www.makeartexeter.com

Underground exploring →

Fascinating Facts

⭐ The underground passages were designed so the water pipes serving the city would be easy to mend if anything happened to them. In most towns, when a pipe gets blocked, it has to be dug up. In Exeter, people used to just follow the underground passages to the source of the problem and deal with it easily.

Top Tip

Download a relic trail from the website before you visit. It contains all kinds of challenges to complete during your trip.

When does walking give you wet feet?

When you have a spring in your step!

PLAN YOUR VISIT 3

Exeter's Underground Passages

2 Paris Street, Exeter, EX1 1GA

www.exeter.gov.uk/passages

📞 **01392 665 887**

🕐 **Mon-Sat (peak) 09.30-17.30 & Sun 10.30-16.00**
Opening hours vary throughout year

£

I want to go here ☐

BE PULLED ALONG BY A HORSE

...on The Grand Western Canal

Horses aren't a common form of transport these days. They're slower than cars and difficult to keep in a garage. However, they used to be the best way of getting around, particularly if you had a canal boat!

The Grand Western Canal meanders for eleven miles from Tiverton to Lowdwells. It's fun to wander alongside the canal, but nothing beats a trip on one of the UK's four remaining horse-drawn barges. We recommend the two-and-a-half-hour return journey, which includes a stop for stretching your legs.

You can pet the horse as it rests under a tree or have a look at the aqueduct and old railway line. Life is never banal when you're on a canal!

Sticker Scores

5 PRETTY HORSE

4 SUPERB STALLION

3 PLEASANT PONY

2 MEDIOCRE MARE

1 PRETTY *HOARSE!*

Best Of The Rest

🔑 You don't have to be pulled by a horse on the canal! You can also hire a Canadian canoe, a motorboat, a rowing boat, or a bike from the farm next door.

Make A Day Of It

🔑 Badger a badger! Tiverton Badger Watch is a evening walk to a local hide where you can see these shy creatures, and also spot owls, mice and woodpeckers.
www.devonbadgerwatch.co.uk

🔑 Check out Tiverton Castle nearby. You can try on English Civil War armour and carry a cannonball.
www.tivertoncastle.com

← One horsepower

Fascinating Facts

★ **The horses used to pull the canals are all heavy horses. This doesn't mean they have a weight problem – heavy horses are big, strong animals that can be relied upon to pull a canal boat at a constant speed.**

★ It's much easier to pull big weights on water. A horse that could move a tonne on land would be able to pull a whopping 40 tonnes in the water. That's why canals were created – they allowed the transportation of heavy goods across long distances.

Photo Op
Take a pic of you patting the horse that pulled you along.

PLAN YOUR VISIT ④

Tiverton Canal Company
The Wharf, Canal Hill, Tiverton, EX16 4HX
www.tivertoncanal.co.uk
📞 01884 253 345
🕐 **Daily (Apr-Oct) timetables vary**

££ ✕

I want to go here ☐

SEE A SIXTEEN-SIDED HOUSE

...at A la Ronde

For most people, four sides to their house is plenty. However, for the Parminter cousins only sixteen sides would do!

A la Ronde was built when Jane and Mary Parminter came back from travelling around Europe. They had got used to the continental weather and wanted a home that made the most of what little English sun there is. So they built a house with sixteen sides and loads of windows to let the sunshine stream in!

A la Ronde's decorations are as eccentric as its design. One room is encrusted with 25,000 shells! And there's plenty to do besides admire the architecture – you can also dress up as a Regency lady or a Victorian gentleman!

Sticker Scores

5 HEAVENLY HEXADECAGON

4 DIVINE DODECAGON

3 OK OCTAGON

2 POOR PENTAGON

1 ALL GONE

Photo Op
See if you can make your own sixteen-sided shape out of twigs on the ground. It's harder than it sounds! Then take a photo of you standing next to it.

Make A Day Of It

 See flying falcons and other animals at the World of Country Life. You can also ride a safari deer train, feed lambs, deer and calves, and walk goats. Oh, and there are also awesome outdoor play areas. www.worldofcountrylife.co.uk

 Scramble through the trees like a monkey! Go Ape in Haldon Forest has an awesome aerial assault course complete with log bridges and aerial runways. Age restrictions apply. www.goape.co.uk

 Bathe on Exmouth Beach. You can also hire a boat, surf the waves, or enjoy a Punch and Judy show in the summer.

← More sides than your average house

Fascinating Facts

★ **The central bit of the house is a hallway known as the Octagon because of its eight-sided shape. It also has eight doors coming off it (one on each side) – each leads to a different room!**

★ The house's walls are nearly one metre thick! That is thicker than most castle walls. Other curious features include sliding doors and hidden seating.

★ **The cousins were determined that their house should only be inherited by women. They specified in their wills that it must pass to unmarried female relatives. In over 200 years, it has had only one male owner!**

PLAN YOUR VISIT ⑤

A la Ronde
Summer Lane, Exmouth, EX8 5BD
www.nationaltrust.org.uk

 01395 265 514

 Sat-Wed (peak) 11.00-17.00
Opening hours vary throughout year

 ££   NT

I want to go here ☐

RIDE ON THE TOP DECK OF A TRAM

...on the Seaton Tramway

In many parts of the world, trams are an important way for people to get from place to place. In Seaton, however, the trams are titchy and just for tourists!

The Seaton Tramway runs along a three-mile track from Seaton to Colyton, alongside the river Axe. All the fourteen trams that run on the line are mini-marvels with their own history and identity. Look out for car fourteen, which started life in 1904 as a working tram in London, or car eight, which is painted bright pink!

If the weather's good, take a seat on the top deck and keep an eye out for wildlife as you trundle along. You should see sheep, rabbits and all kinds of birds. It's a *tram*-endous way to spend a day!

Sticker Scores

5	4	3
TERRIFIC TRAM	TOP TRAIN	CRACKING COACH

2	1
BASIC BUS	BROKEN DOWN

Top Tip

Get an all-day ticket for unlimited travel. Use the spotters guide provided by the ticket office to tick off which trams you've ridden.

Make A Day Of It

 Search for fossils along the Jurassic Coast, an amazing stretch of coastline running through East Devon and Dorset. Many of the coastal cliffs were formed during the Jurassic period up to 200 million years ago. Fossils can still be found on its beaches today – look for bits where the sea has washed away the soft clay and mud.

 Take a tour of the Beer Quarry Caves. Don't worry, despite the name, this isn't a place where miners dug beer out of the ground! Beer is also the name of a place in Devon, and its quarry provided stone for many famous buildings in England.

← The pinkest tram you'll ever see

Fascinating Facts

★ **In 2009 an enormous pliosaur skull was discovered on the Jurassic coast. The head alone measures over two metres – that's longer than most adult men! Pliosaurs lived 150 million years ago and are the largest sea reptiles that have ever existed. They could grow up to twelve metres long.**

★ The Seaton tramway has a narrow-gauge track, which means it's thinner than normal trams or trains. The two rails are just 61 centimetres apart, whereas most trams run on rails that are at least 100 centimetres apart.

★ **Many of the trams have cool reversible seats. You can move the seat forward or backwards to change the direction you're facing.**

PLAN YOUR VISIT ⑥

Seaton Tramway

Seaton Terminus, Underfleet Car Park, Seaton, EX12 2TB

www.tram.co.uk

📞 **01297 20375**

🕐 **Daily (Feb-Dec) timetables vary**

££

I want to go here ☐

NORTH DEVON

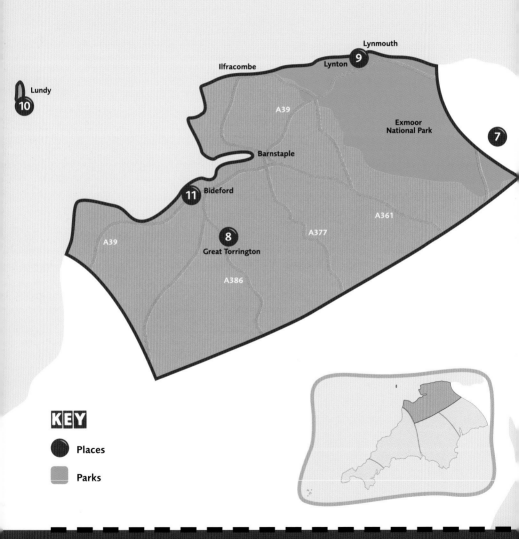

KEY

● Places

▮ Parks

EAST DEVON

NORTH DEVON

SOUTH DEVON

CENTRAL CORNWALL

WEST CORNWALL

TOP FIVES

GO ON A LAND ROVER SAFARI

...at Barle Valley Safaris

Exmoor is not an obvious Safari spot. There are no lions or zebras roaming around, and it's less sunny than Africa. However, we think a Barle Valley safari is still a great way to spot British wildlife . . .

Barle Valley Safaris operate from Dulverton and Dunster. You board a Land Rover and an expert will guide you to places where you can see red deer, Exmoor ponies and other intriguing animals.

The tours last three hours and involve driving off-road, fording through rivers, and marvelling at mysterious monuments. You need at least two passengers to travel . . . but we think the *moor* the merrier!

Sticker Scores

⭐ 5	⭐ 4	⭐ 3
DELIGHTFUL DEER	SPLENDID STAG	PRETTY PONY

⭐ 2	⭐ 1
HAIRY HORSE	*SAFARI* SO GOOD

Make A Day Of It

🔑 Explore Exmoor by foot, on horseback, or on a bike. Visit www.exmoor-nationalpark.gov.uk for recommended walks and rides.

🔑 See how honey is made! Quince Honey Farm is England's largest, with 1,500 hives. You can learn about how bees live and why they make honey, and even sample some of the produce . . . it's the bee's knees!

What do you call a deer with no eyes?

No *eye-deer*!

What do you call a deer with no eyes and no legs?

Still no *eye-deer*!

← Don't try this in your family's car

Fascinating Facts

⭐ **Exmoor ponies are the oldest British pony, and have been running wild on Exmoor since ancient times. They are classed as a rare breed – fewer than 1,200 are left.**

⭐ Most male deer (including the red deer on Exmoor) have antlers, but not all year round. They fall off every spring and grow back in the summer.

⭐ **There are carnivorous plants on Exmoor! Exmoor's soil is acidic and does not contain many nutrients, so the sundew plant seeks its food from passing insects. Sticky tentacles trap flies which are then swiftly digested. We'd rather have a burger!**

PLAN YOUR VISIT 7

Barle Valley Safaris

Goosemoor Station Cottage, Wheddon Cross, Minehead, Somerset, TA24 7BY

www.exmoorwildlifesafaris.co.uk

📞 **01643 851386**

🕐 **Daily 09.00-18.00
Advance booking required**

£££

I want to go here ☐

WIELD AN ANCIENT WEAPON

...at Torrington 1646

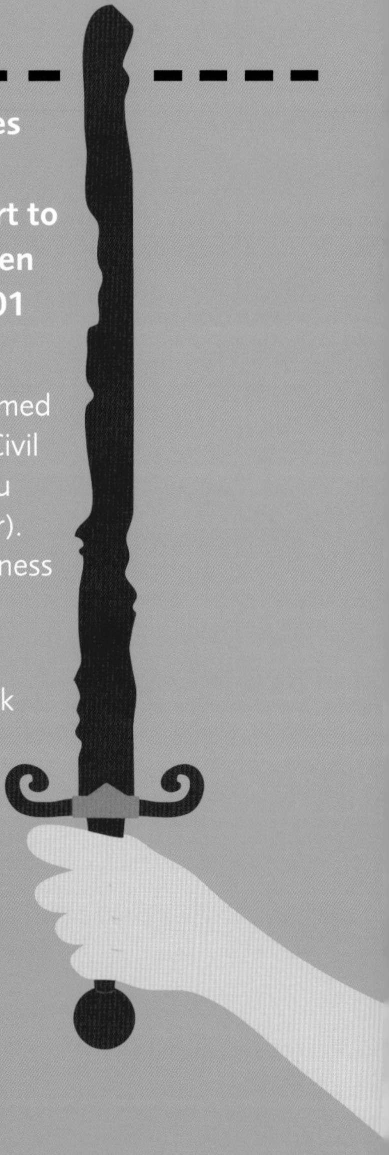

Historical museums can sometimes be boring. However, Torrington 1646 is pure entertainment from start to finish. After all, it's hard to yawn when a man called Sir Basil is explaining 101 uses for wee!

Torrington 1646 is an attraction where costumed actors tell you about life during the English Civil War. There are weaponry displays where you can learn how to use a pike (a pole-like spear). You may also see muskets being fired, or witness a sword fight – just don't get in the way!

As well as the weapons, you get a chance to dress up in armour and find a witch. We think it's a mystery that history is not always this enjoyable!

Sticker Scores

5 AVENGING ARROW

4 POINTY PIKE

3 SHARP SWORD

2 BRUTAL BATTERING RAM

1 FEATHER DUSTER

Make A Day Of It

 Go to a fun shopping centre.
Atlantic Village in Bideford includes
a massive (free) playground with
bungee trampolines, adventure golf
and a pirate galleon. So you can play
whilst grown-ups pay!

 Hunt with a falcon. At North
Devon Falconry, you can learn how
to handle Harris hawks (a hunting
bird). Advance booking is required.

← "Chaaarrrrgggggeeeeee!"

Photo Op
Take a photo of you
stuck in Torrington's
stocks!

Fascinating Facts

★ **There really were many different
uses for urine in the 1600s. Housewives
used it as a form of bleach to make
clothes white. Some people put it on
their skin to remove chilblains. And it
also was once the main ingredient in
gunpowder!** *Wee* **think that we'd rather
just flush it down the toilet . . .**

★ In the 1600s it was fashionable for
women to have big bums. So, to make their
backside look broader, some would attach
something called a bum roll. This was a roll
of material that padded out the posterior!

★ **The expression 'cock up' (meaning
to mess something up) comes from
misfiring muskets (old-fashioned
guns). The firing device on a musket
is called the cock and if it fails to fire
it jams in an upright position!**

PLAN YOUR VISIT ⓼

Torrington 1646
Castle Hill, South Street, Great Torrington,
EX38 8AA

www.torrington-1646.co.uk

☎ **01805 626146**

🕐 **Mon-Fri (peak): tours run 10.00-14.00
(allow 2 hours)**

££ ✗ 🎁

I want to go here ☐

TRAVEL ON A FUNICULAR

...on the Lynton and Lynmouth Cliff Railway

There are two ways to get from Lynmouth to Lynton. Either you can wind your way along the steep roads joining the two tiny towns. Or you can take the direct route and travel up this phenomenal funicular!

Lynton and Lynmouth are villages on an amazing stretch of Devon coastline. Drive in along the A39 from Minehead and your car will be right on the cliff edge – so make sure the driver is concentrating!

No visit is complete without a ride on the cool cliff railway (also called a funicular). It's the steepest in Europe and runs on water power. Gravity helps to move the two cars – as one descends, the other is pulled upwards. If you like unusual journeys, you'll love this funicular in particular!

Sticker Scores

5 FUN-ICULAR   **4** VAN-TASTIC   **3** BICY-COOL

2 SORRY LORRY   **1** CAR-TASTROPHE

Make A Day Of It

🔑 See a wonderful waterfall. Glen Lyn Gorge is a beautiful spot for a walk alongside some ferocious falls. It's 77 metres to the top – that's coincidentally the amount by which the sea level will rise if all the ice in the world melts.

🔑 Visit the Power of Water exhibition at the bottom of the Glen Lyn Gorge. Press the button on the Archimedes Screw and watch how you can make water travel uphill!

🔑 Feast on fish and chips beside Lynmouth Harbour. There are a couple of restaurants offering cracking seaside suppers.

← It's steeper than it looks

Fascinating Facts

★ Before the funicular was built, people had great trouble getting between Lynton and Lynmouth. Donkeys and horses used to transport people and cargo up the cliff paths, but the journey was so demanding that they had a very short working life.

★ Lynmouth suffered a terrible flood in 1952. 229 millimetres of rain fell in a day and 34 people died in the tragedy. 100 buildings were destroyed, along with most of the village's bridges.

★ More water gushes down Glen Lyn Gorge in one night than flows through the river Thames in London in one month!

PLAN YOUR VISIT 9

Lynton and Lynmouth Cliff Railway

The Esplanade, Lynmouth, EX35 6EQ
www.cliffrailwaylynton.co.uk

📞 01598 753908

🕐 Daily (Aug) 10.00-21.00
Daily (Peak) 10.00-19.00
Closing times vary throughout year

£

I want to go here ☐

GET LOST ON AN ISOLATED ISLAND

...at Lundy Island (from Ilfracombe)

Don't worry, we're not suggesting you get permanently lost! Lundy is small enough that no matter where you are on the island you'll never be lost for long.

Lundy is situated about twelve miles off the North Devon coast. It has had an eventful past – it was used by the Vikings, then was popular with pirates, and even once had its own king!

There's plenty to do on a visit to Lundy. You can explore ancient Celtic gravestones, peer at unusual plants and animals, look at a lighthouse and see the remains of a German bomber aircraft. We suggest you go by boat and stay the night on the campsite or in the lighthouse. We can't think of a better place to get lost!

Sticker Scores

5 INVITING ISLAND

4 AMAZING ARCHIPELAGO

3 PRETTY PROMONTORY

2 PLAIN PENINSULA

1 TRAFFIC ISLAND

Make A Day Of It

 Scoff delicious scones at the St James Tea Room in Ilfracombe after your visit. They are freshly baked on site. *Mmm!*

 Watermouth Bay has a fantastic beach if you want to follow your island adventure with some seaside fun.

Similar Spot

Looe Island, off the south coast of Cornwall, is another pretty little island. Most people go there by boat, but at very low tides you can sometimes walk to it! www.looeisland.co.uk

← Look out for goats on Lundy

Top Tip

You can swim with seals off Lundy Island by taking a Clovelly Charters boat trip. Bring goggles, a mask and a wetsuit.

Fascinating Facts

★ **Lundy island only has around 30 residents. So you needn't worry about getting caught up in rush hour traffic!**

★ The island is three miles long and under a mile wide, so you can nearly always work out where you are.

★ **Despite having hardly any residents, Lundy has its own stamps! They were introduced by King Harman in 1929 to pay for distributing the post. They are still printed today, so you can send a friend a Lundy-stamped postcard during your visit!**

★ During the winter there's no regular boat service, so a helicopter runs between the mainland and the island instead.

PLAN YOUR VISIT 10

Lundy Island

off Devon coast (ship sails from Ilfracombe and Bideford)

www.lundyisland.co.uk

📞 01271 863636

🕐 **Selected days Mar-Nov
Check website for timetable**

£££ (day trip)

I want to go here ☐

WATCH SHEEPDOGS HERD SHEEP

...at The Big Sheep

There's more to this place than bleating balls of fluff. They've got a farm, a play area and even a battlefield. We think you'd be *baaa*-king mad not to visit!

The Big Sheep is a a sheep-themed attraction – and we love it! You can see a sheep-shearing session, watch a sheepdog show and even cuddle sheepdog puppies!

What do you get if you cross a sheep and a kangaroo?

A woolly jumper!

Away from the sheep you can ride a horse, take a tractor around the farm, pedal on go-karts and catapult water balloons at your family! We particularly like Battlefield Live, where you get to shoot lasers across a large open battlefield. So don't be *sheep*-ish – *ewe* would be mad not to visit!

Sticker Scores

5 LOVELY LAMB

4 MARVELLOUS MUTTON

3 GORGEOUS GOAT

2 STANDARD SHEEP

1 *LAMB*-ENTABLE

Make A Day Of It

 Scramble on an assault course. Next door to The Big Sheep is The Ultimate High, a rope-and-wood assault course high off the ground. www.theultimatehigh.com

 Go to a Gnome Reserve. Borrow a hat and a fishing rod and walk amongst over 1,000 garden gnomes! www.gnomereserve.co.uk

Photo Op

Have your photo taken before and after you go on Battlefield Live. We guarantee you'll be muddier in the 'after' photo!

← Battlefield Live (not herding sheep):

Fascinating Facts

⭐ **Candles were once made out of sheep's fat! Tallow (the proper name for sheep's blubber) has also been used as the basis for soap. However we definitely don't advise taking a leg of lamb into the shower!**

⭐ Sheep have long tails when they are born. These are usually cut off when they are young to stop the tails getting clogged with sheep poo. Apparently sheep are not big fans of toilet paper!

⭐ **The most famous sheep in the world is called Dolly. She was created in 1996 through a process called cloning. This means she was not born naturally, but grown by scientists using cells from another sheep.**

PLAN YOUR VISIT ⑪

The Big Sheep

Abbotsham, EX39 5AP

www.thebigsheep.co.uk

📞 01237 472366

🕐 Daily (peak) 10.00-18.00
Sat-Sun (out of season) 10.00-17.00

£££ (peak) **££** (out of season)

I want to go here ☐

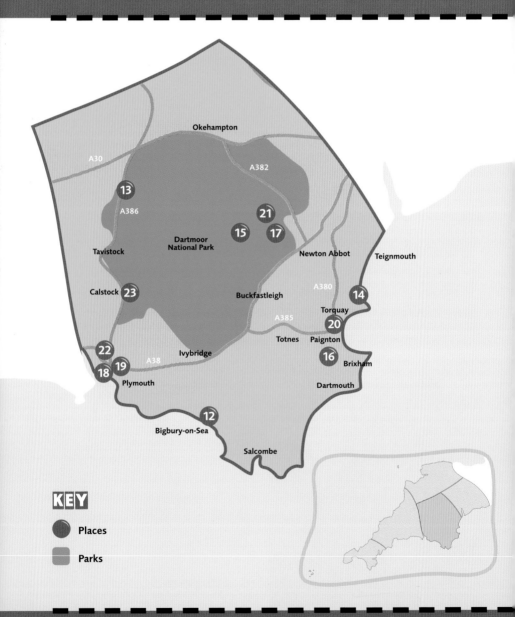

Okehampton

A30

13

A386

21

15   17

Dartmoor
National Park

Tavistock

Newton Abbot   Teignmouth

A380

Calstock 23   14

Buckfastleigh   Torquay

A385   20

Totnes   Paignton

22

Ivybridge   16

19   A38   Brixham

18

Plymouth   Dartmouth

12

Bigbury-on-Sea

Salcombe

A382

KEY

● Places

■ Parks

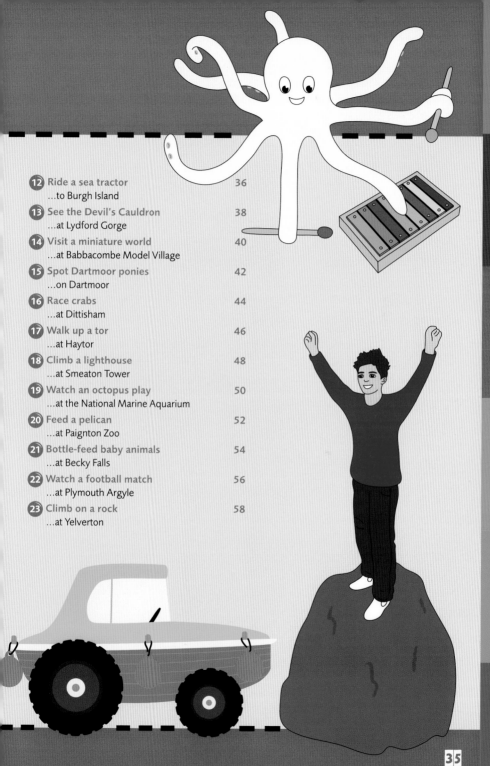

EAST DEVON

NORTH DEVON

SOUTH DEVON

CENTRAL CORNWALL

WEST CORNWALL

TOP FIVES

RIDE A SEA TRACTOR

...to Burgh Island

Boats bob on water. Tractors travel over ground. But how do you take a trip across both land AND sea? Well, here's one idea – use a sea tractor!

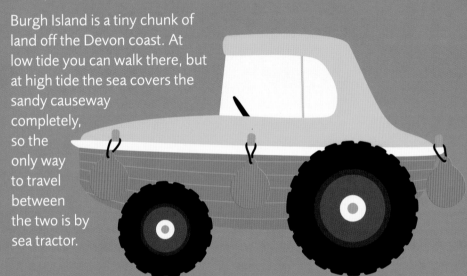

Burgh Island is a tiny chunk of land off the Devon coast. At low tide you can walk there, but at high tide the sea covers the sandy causeway completely, so the only way to travel between the two is by sea tractor.

Sticker Scores

5 SEA TRACTOR	**4** FANTASTIC FERRY	**3** COLOSSAL CAUSEWAY
2 DINGY DINGHY	**1** SUNK TRACTOR	

Although the sea tractor is owned by the Burgh Island Hotel, visitors are welcome to use it. You trundle along on a raised platform with waves lapping beneath you. Once on the island, search for the remains of the old chapel. We think this day out with a tractor has a real wow factor!

Make A Day Of It

← The Burgh Island sea tractor

🔑 Have fun on the beach at Bigbury-on-Sea. The sea tractor departs from this seaside village, which has one of Devon's nicest beaches. Build sandcastles, explore the rock pools, paddle in the water or munch on food at the beach café.

Photo Op
Take a picture of you sitting on the tractor while it's driving through the waves.

How did the farmer find his lost cow?
He *tractor* down!

Fascinating Facts

★ **The sea tractor was designed by a nuclear scientist called Robert Jackson in 1969 and is the only one of its kind. His only payment was a case of champagne!**

★ The world's biggest tractor is the Challenger MT975-B. Its engine produces a hefty 600 horsepower, and the tractor weighs a terrifying 27 tonnes. That's as heavy as 50 horses (but more useful when ploughing a field)!

★ **The Challenger MT975-B is powerful enough to lift about five times its own weight, but that still makes it ten times less powerful than an ant. Ants can lift up to 50 times their own weight!**

PLAN YOUR VISIT 12

Burgh Island Hotel
Burgh Island, Kingsbridge, TQ7 4BG
www.burghisland.com

📞 01548 810 514

🕐 Daily (peak) 10.00-18.00
Daily (out of season) 10.00-17.00

£

I want to go here ☐

37

SEE THE DEVIL'S CAULDRON

...at Lydford Gorge

Hell is supposed to be full of flames, so you may be surprised to find out that this cauldron is actually part of a roaring river. We think the Devil would struggle to serve up a stew here, but it is a *stirring* sight!

The Devil's Cauldron is a wonderful whirlpool that's the highlight of a walk along Lydford Gorge. Start off at the National Trust building and walk down into the gorge. As you approach the Devil's Cauldron, the path gets narrower and the river gets louder. Hold onto the rail beside the stone steps so you don't fall in!

There's plenty more to see along the gorge – look out for brown trout at Tucker's Pool and spot dormice boxes along the trail. *Gorge*-ous!

Sticker Scores

5 DEVIL'S CAULDRON

4 BEELZEBUB'S BUCKET

3 SATAN'S SAUCEPAN

2 MONSTER'S MUG

1 SISSY'S SAUCER

Top Tip

Wear sturdy shoes for your descent to the Devil's Cauldron. The path can be slippery and you wouldn't want to end up as part of the Devil's stew . . .

Best Of The Rest

 Wonder at the Whitelady Waterfall, where the water plunges down a dramatic, 30-metre drop.

 Zoom down the zip wire in the adventure playground, near the National Trust building.

Fascinating Facts

★ There are lots of attractions calling themselves the Devil's Cauldron around the world. It's the name of a weird rock chamber in Wales and a spooky pool of boiling-hot water in Nevada in the USA. Thankfully none of them are actually home to demonic chefs!

Make A Day Of It

 Go to jail at Dartmoor Prison. Its museum collection includes things made illegally by inmates and ancient items used to restrain people. www.dartmoor-prison.co.uk

 Go down a pit at Morwellham Quay. Take the mine train alongside the river Tamar, before going deep underground in the copper mine. www.morwellham-quay.co.uk

 Stroke a donkey! Tamar Valley Donkey Park and Sanctuary has donkeys, goats, sheep, pigs, rabbits and guinea pigs which you can pet and feed. There's also an indoor play barn for rainy days. www.donkeypark.com

← The Whitelady Waterfall in Lydford Gorge

SOUTH DEVON

PLAN YOUR VISIT 13

Lydford Gorge
Lydford, Nr. Tavistock, EX20 4BH
www.nationaltrust.org.uk/lydfordgorge
📞 **01822 820320**
🕐 **Opening hours vary throughout year**
£ **NT**

I want to go here ☐

VISIT A MINIATURE WORLD

...at Babbacombe Model Village

Have you ever wondered what it feels like to be a giant? Well, you'll find out at Babbacombe as you peer down at the miniature models below.

Babbacombe Model Village is home to over 400 miniature houses, shops, restaurants, cinemas and landmarks (including Stonehenge). There's even a massive castle, complete with fire-breathing dragon!

Look out for all the sneakily hidden items when you visit. Depending on the time of year you might find Wally (from *Where's Wally?*), red herrings and dinosaur eggs dotted around the grounds. The owners also adjust the scenery to suit the time of year – so there's a covering of snow at Christmas time. The models may be mini, but we think this place is big fun!

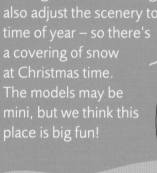

Sticker Scores

5 — MINI METROPOLIS

4 — CRAMPED CITY

3 — SMALL SUBURB

2 — TINY TOWN

1 — HUMBLE HAMLET

Photo Op

Take a close-up of one of the scenes at Babbacombe then see if you can fool people into thinking it wasn't taken in a model village!

Best Of The Rest

🔑 Watch a 4D film. Babbacombe has a fantastic 4D cinema. It's a bit like a 3D cinema, but with moving seats, flashing lights and super sound effects.

Make A Day Of It

🔑 Ride on a cliff railway down to nearby Oddicombe Beach. The steep funicular railway runs down the cliffs to a brilliant beach.

🔑 Creep through a prehistoric cave at Kents Cavern. Travel 400 million years back in time, then have a go at cave painting, brass rubbing and tribal face marking.

← Attack!

Fascinating Facts

⭐ **The world's smallest house is probably one designed by the Tumbleweed Tiny House Company. One of their pint-sized creations covers just six square metres. That means it's about as wide as an adult, and as long as two eleven year olds. Your bathroom is probably bigger!**

Top Tip
Your ticket to Babbacombe allows you to go there as many times as you want in the same day, so why not visit again during the evening and see the village illuminated at night?

PLAN YOUR VISIT 14

Babbacombe Model Village
Off St Marychurch Road, Torquay, TQ1 4PR
www.model-village.co.uk

📞 **01803 328669**

🕐 **Daily (Peak) 10.00-22.30**
Opening hours vary throughout year

££

I want to go here ☐

SPOT DARTMOOR PONIES

...on Dartmoor

Dartmoor is home to two famous populations: prisoners and ponies. You're unlikely to spot the inmates, as they're all (hopefully) housed inside Dartmoor prison. But anyway, we think the ponies are the *mane* attraction!

The Dartmoor pony has been around for 1,000 years. Despite its small size it's a very tough breed because it has had to get used to the unfriendly weather. These heroic horses used to carry tin across the moor from the nearby mines, and were even used in Dartmoor prison!

Sticker Scores

5 DIVINE DARTMOOR

4 EXCELLENT EXMOOR

3 AVERAGE ARABIAN

2 TIRED THOROUGHBRED

1 DEPRESSED DONKEY

When you're out walking on the moors you'll see small herds of ponies roaming about. Try looking around Widecombe-in-the-Moor, or Dartmeet. Wild horses couldn't drag us away!

What's black and white and eats like a horse?
A zebra!

Best Of The Rest

🔑 Take a horseback trek across the moor, starting at a local riding school. Check www.discoverdartmoor.co.uk for a full list of Dartmoor stables.

Similar Spots

🔑 Visit a donkey sanctuary. The sanctuary at Sidmouth has rescued donkeys of all descriptions – over 13,000 since it first started. www.thedonkeysanctuary.org.uk

🔑 See a mini pony. The Miniature Pony Centre has ponies and donkeys plus an awesome adventure playground. www.miniatureponycentre.com

← Yaaaawwwwwwwwn!

Fascinating Facts

⭐ **Technically, Dartmoor's ponies aren't wild, as they are usually owned by local farmers. But they can roam around freely and eat and drink whatever they want, which sounds pretty *wild* to us!**

⭐ Each September, farmers get together and round up the ponies. This event is called a drift and is a big deal locally. People on bikes, horses and two feet round up the ponies then hand them over to their owners.

Top Tip

Do not feed the ponies. It may seem friendly, but it encourages them to come close to the roads, and that can lead to them being killed by cars.

PLAN YOUR VISIT 15

Dartmoor
www.dartmoor-npa.gov.uk
FREE

I want to go here ☐

RACE CRABS

...at Dittisham

You don't need complicated kit to go crabbing. All you need is a long piece of string, some bait (we like bacon), a net and a bucket to put the crabs in.

Dittisham is a village with a pretty pontoon. Park at Greenway and take the passenger ferry across. If it isn't already waiting you can ring the bell and the ferry will come to fetch you.

Sit on the pontoon and lower your string (with bait attached) into the water until it hits the sea floor. Wait a few minutes then pull your line gently up to the surface.

Hopefully a crab will be hanging on. We like to catch a couple and race them. See if you can guess which one will win!

Sticker Scores

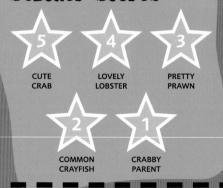

★ 5	★ 4	★ 3
CUTE CRAB	LOVELY LOBSTER	PRETTY PRAWN

★ 2	★ 1
COMMON CRAYFISH	CRABBY PARENT

Why do mussels and crabs never share anything?
Because they're *shell*-fish!

44

Make A Day Of It

🗝 Explore Dartmouth Castle. This pretty castle sits on the mouth of the river Dart. Take a boat trip from Dartmouth quay. www.english-heritage.org.uk

🗝 Ride a train and a boat. The Dartmouth Steam Railway and Riverboat Company offers a range of boat and rail options. Summer days out include the Pirate Pet's Adventures and a cool crabbing competition! www.dartmouthrailriver.co.uk

🗝 See a real pirate ship in Brixham. The village is home to a replica of the explorer Francis Drake's swashbuckling ship, the *Golden Hind*. www.goldenhind.co.uk

← "Got one!"

Similar Spots

🗝 Here are some perfect places to use your line:

Padstow in Cornwall (see p70) has a steep-sided harbour which is ideal for crabbing.

Teignmouth in Devon is home to a crab-tastic harbour with a colourful row of houses in the background.

Wembury (near Plymouth) has some fantastic rock pools where you can find all kinds of shellfish. Wembury Marine Centre hosts rock-pool rambles during the summer.

SOUTH DEVON

PLAN YOUR VISIT 16

Greenway Quay
Greenway Road, Greenway, TQ5 0ES
www.greenwayferry.co.uk

📞 **01803 882 811**

🕐 **Mon-Fri 08.00-18.00**
Sat-Sun 09.00-18.00
Last ferry out of season is at 16.30

FREE (crabbing) **£** (ferry)

I want to go here ☐

WALK UP A TOR

...at Haytor

Tor is the local Dartmoor word to describe a hill. You'll find loads of them across the moor, but our favourite is Haytor.

Haytor is 457 metres above sea level, and has amazing views down to the Teign Estuary. Start your walk at the information centre, where the staff will suggest a route depending on how energetic you're feeling! There's normally an ice-cream van here, so you can begin (or end) your trek with a tasty treat.

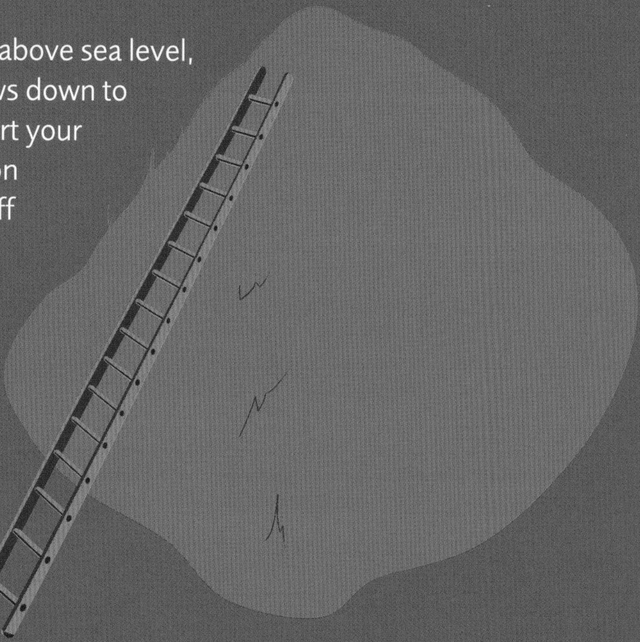

Sticker Scores

5 TERRIFFIC TOR

4 HONEST HILL

3 SATISFACTORY SLOPE

2 HUMBLE HUMMOCK

1 *TOR*-TURE!

Keep a look out for ponies (see p42) as you climb to the summit. Then when you reach the top, have fun climbing over the impressive outcrops of Haytor Rocks. It's *tor*-iffic!

Photo Op
Stand on one of the Haytor Rocks and hold your arms above your head in celebration at reaching the top.

Make A Day Of It

🔑 Go to a toy and games factory! The House of Marbles is a working glass and games factory in a pottery. Wander around the old kilns and check out the marble-tastic museum. www.houseofmarbles.com

> ### Top Tip
> The Rock Inn nearby does great food – it's the perfect place for a spot of lunch before or after your trek up the tor!

Fascinating Facts

★ A tramway used to transport granite rocks from Haytor Quarry towards building sites around the country. Haytor granite was used to make London Bridge and the British Museum. The last stone was dug in 1919, but you can still see parts of the tramway today.

★ Letterboxing is the name for a popular Dartmoor hobby. It involves searching for hundreds of hidden letterboxes using clues to their locations. Each letterbox has a stamp inside so you can prove you've been there. Visit www.dartmoor-npa.gov.uk for more information.

← Haytor in the snow

PLAN YOUR VISIT 17
Haytor Visitor Centre
Nr. Haytor Vale on B3387, TQ13
www.dartmoor-npa.gov.uk
📞 **01364 661520**
FREE

I want to go here ☐

CLIMB A LIGHTHOUSE

...at Smeaton's Tower

Lighthouses are normally placed beside dangerous rocks so that ships can steer round them. So you might well wonder what Smeaton's Tower is doing on Plymouth Hoe, well away from the path of seafaring ships . . .

The answer is that Smeaton's Tower only arrived in its current location in 1877. Before then it stood at the treacherous Eddystone Rocks, fourteen miles out to sea. It was moved when the rocks beneath it were found to be unstable and has stood on the Hoe ever since.

Today you can climb all 93 steps to the top of the tower. Once there you have an amazing view out to the current Eddystone Lighthouse, which still stops ships being smashed on the rocks to this day.

Sticker Scores

5 LIGHTHOUSE

4 TREE HOUSE

3 WENDY HOUSE

2 GREENHOUSE

1 MADHOUSE

Make A Day Of It

🔑 Swim in a seaside lido. Tinside Pool is an awesome open-air spot next to Smeaton's Tower. It's a delightful place for a dip!

🔑 Take a ferry to a smugglers' park. Mount Edgcumbe used to be a smuggling base, but now it's known for its great gardens and cracking country house. Travel there on the Cremyll Ferry, which departs from Admiral's Hard in Stonehouse. www.mountedgcumbe.gov.uk

Top Tip
Don't miss Britain's largest fireworks competition on the Hoe every August. It's a sparkling day out! www.britishfireworks.co.uk

Fascinating Facts

⭐ **The first Eddystone Lighthouse was destroyed during a storm in 1703. Henry Winstanley (the engineer who built it) was so sure it would survive that he was visiting at the time. Sadly he was wrong . . .**

⭐ Lighthouse number two burned down in a massive fire in 1755. The lead around the light melted and some of it fell into the mouth of the unlucky keeper, Henry Hall. He died a few days later.

⭐ **Smeaton's Tower (lighthouse number three) was built in 1756 by John Smeaton. He was inspired by oak trees and built the tower in a circular shape using bricks. Its foundations still stand next to lighthouse number four today.**

PLAN YOUR VISIT 18

Smeaton's Tower
The Hoe, Plymouth, PL1 2NZ
www.plymouth.gov.uk
📞 01752 304774
🕐 Tue-Sat 10.00-12.00 & 13.00-15.00
£

I want to go here ☐

← Smeaton's Tower

WATCH AN OCTOPUS PLAY

...at the National Marine Aquarium

You don't need a theatre (or actors) to watch an octopus play! All you need is to go down to the National Marine Aquarium in Plymouth, where you can see Bagpipe the octopus playing with his toys.

The National Marine Aquarium is full of fascinating creatures – they have everything from sharks to sea horses. Walk through the warm tropical sea section, then look out for local Plymouth species.

We particularly like octopus playtime, where you can watch Bagpipe playing with a ball and other toys. He can even open a jar to get his lunch! We promise there's nothing *fishy* going on – this is one seriously talented creature!

Sticker Scores

⭐ **5** AWESOME OCTOPUS

⭐ **4** SMASHING SHARK

⭐ **3** GREAT GOLDFISH

⭐ **2** REASONABLE RAY

⭐ **1** MEASLY MINNOW

Top Tip

Once you've bought your ticket, you can come back as many times as you like in a twelve month period.

Best Of The Rest

 Check out the jellyfish nursery. These strange creatures have no heart or brain, and use their stinging tentacles to catch food.

Make A Day Of It

 See the Mayflower Steps on the Barbican. The Barbican is one of the few parts of Plymouth to escape bombing during World War Two. The Mayflower Steps, opposite the aquarium, were the departure point for the Pilgrim Fathers – people who travelled from Plymouth to America in the 1600s and helped set up the country.

Why do octopuses make good soldiers?

Because they're well-*armed*!

← Staring at fish

Fascinating Facts

★ **The most poisonous jellyfish in the world is a form of box jellyfish known as the sea wasp. Each individual creature contains enough venom to kill 60 adult humans!**

★ Octopuses have eight legs and three hearts, but no bones. They can change the colour of their bodies and squirt ink at predators trying to attack them.

Top Tip

Sleep with sharks! The aquarium does summer sleepovers, so you can literally sleep with (or at least next to) the fantastic fish.

PLAN YOUR VISIT 19

The National Marine Aquarium

Rope Walk, Coxside, Plymouth, PL4 0LF

www.national-aquarium.co.uk

📞 0844 893 7938

🕐 Daily (peak) 10.00-18.00
Daily (out of season) 10.00-17.00

££

I want to go here ☐

FEED A PELICAN

...at Paignton Zoo

There are no pelican crossings at Paignton Zoo . . . and, if you follow our advice and feed them fish, there won't be any cross pelicans either!

Paignton has a big zoo with fantastic feeding sessions. Time your visit right and you'll see baboons, elephants and big cats being fed. Just don't get too close – unless you want to end up on the menu! You can even feed pelicans yourself by throwing them fish. These spectacular sea birds have a large throat pouch which they use to catch their lunch.

Once you've had your fill of feeding, there's also a mini-train ride, a jungle bridge and two excellent outdoor playgrounds to keep you entertained. It's our idea of *zoo*-topia!

Sticker Scores

5 PECKISH PELICAN

4 THIRSTY TOUCAN

3 HUNGRY HERON

2 GREEDY GANNET

1 BIRD POO

Best Of The Rest

🔑 Take the Clennon Gorge Nature Trail. This is an enjoyable woodland walk – look out for yellow-necked mice, emperor dragonflies, badgers and buzzards.

Make A Day Of It

🔑 Visit Paignton Sands. The long sandy beach has a pleasure pier with rides and snacks.

🔑 Play pirate-themed crazy golf at Pirates Bay Adventure Golf Course on the seafront. It's great fun, me hearties!

🔑 Slide around at Quaywest Waterpark. *Water* great way to spend a sunny day!

Fascinating Facts

⭐ Pelicans often fish in groups. They get in a line and force fish into shallow water by slapping their wings on the surface and making a loud noise. Once the fish are cornered, they scoop them up in their big throat pouches. We're glad we can just pop to the supermarket when we're peckish!

Top Tip

Paignton Zoo runs activity weeks in August during which you can learn about how to look after the animals. Check the website for details.

← Not a pelican

Why do pelicans carry fish in their beaks? Because they don't have any pockets!

PLAN YOUR VISIT 20

Paignton Zoo Environmental Park

Totnes Road, Paignton, TQ4 7EU

www.paigntonzoo.org.uk

📞 0844 474 2222

🕐 Opens at 10.00 (closing times vary)

£££

I want to go here ☐

BOTTLE-FEED BABY ANIMALS

...at Becky Falls

Becky Falls has been designated an area of special scientific interest, a World Wildlife Fund top site and an area of outstanding natural beauty. We also designate it a delightful Dartmoor day out!

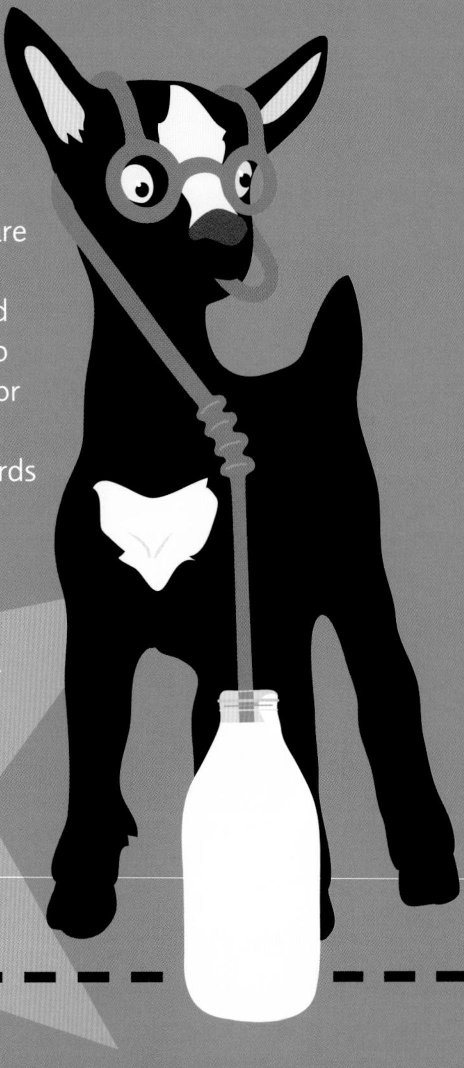

Becky Falls is a wonderful woodland park next to a beautiful waterfall. As well as admiring the gushing falls you can also feed animals, meet bunnies and guinea pigs, and stare at creepy-crawlies. There's also an indoor theatre, plus woodland to scramble through and rivers to get soaked in. And if you're up for a challenge, take the children's letterboxing trail – free stamp cards are provided by the gift shop.

Sticker Scores

5 BECKY FALLS

4 ANGEL FALLS

3 NIAGARA FALLS

2 VICTORIA FALLS

1 BECKY FALLS OVER

Make A Day Of It

🔑 See mini ponies! The *neigh*-bouring miniature pony centre is perfect if you like horses. You can see Shetlands, delight at donkeys, watch birds of prey, and even ride a pony. It's also got indoor and outdoor adventure playgrounds, an assault course, trampolines and a zip line. www.miniatureponycentre.com

Top Tip
Visit in the springtime and you'll be able to admire the beautiful blooming bluebells!

Fascinating Facts

⭐ **The world's tallest waterfall is Angel Falls in Venezuela. It's an astonishing 979 metres high, which is the same as 750 eleven year olds standing on each other's shoulders (but less likely to topple over!).**

⭐ The world's largest waterfall is Victoria Falls, on the border between Zambia and Zimbabwe. It's 1,708 metres wide and 108 metres high. Its local name translates as the 'smoke that thunders', which is a pretty good description of what it looks and sounds like!

SOUTH DEVON

← You can cuddle the animals too

PLAN YOUR VISIT 21

Becky Falls Woodland Park
Manaton, Newton Abbot, TQ13 9UG
www.beckyfalls.com

📞 **01647 221259**

🕐 **Daily (peak) 10.00-17.00**

££

I want to go here ☐

WATCH A FOOTBALL MATCH

...at Plymouth Argyle

Plymouth Argyle are known as the Green Army. But don't worry, the team is not full of pea-coloured aliens! Green is just the colour of their kit . . .

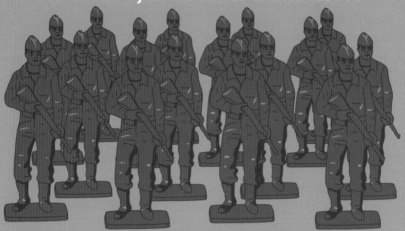

Plymouth is the largest city in the UK to have a football side that has never played in the top division. That may not sound like something to shout about, but we love the local team! The Premiership might be full of global superstars, but in our opinion seeing a match live beats watching it on the telly every time. You get swept away by the roar of the crowd and you can see every kick, pass and push. Wear something green to blend in and cheer on the pride of Plymouth!

Sticker Scores

5 GREEN ARMY

4 PURPLE PLATOON

3 MAROON MILITIA

2 SCARLET SOLDIER

1 RED HERRING

Similar Spots

🔑 Exeter City are another local league club. Like Newcastle United, their stadium is in the city centre and called St James Park. We'll leave you to decide if the quality of Exeter's football is also on a par with Newcastle!
www.exetercityfc.co.uk

🔑 Torquay United are in Devon too, and play at Plainmoor. Sadly there are no league clubs in Cornwall.
www.torquayunited.com

Photo Op

Take a snap of you wearing a Plymouth shirt or scarf. For the full fan effect, you could even paint your face green!

← One of the Green Army!

Fascinating Facts

⭐ **Plymouth Argyle are also known as the Pilgrims. This is a reference to the Pilgrim Fathers – people who left Plymouth for America hundreds of years ago and settled in the country. However, some fans feel like pilgrims today – Plymouth is the most southern league team in the country, so every away game involves a trek up north!**

⭐ Plymouth's most successful season was in 1983-1984, when they reached the semi-finals of the FA Cup. Their other memorable cup run in 2007 ended at the quarter-finals. On both occasions they were beaten by Watford, so the London club is now pretty unpopular with the locals!

PLAN YOUR VISIT 22

Plymouth Argyle
Home Park, Plymouth, PL2 3DQ
www.pafc.co.uk
📞 01752 562 561
£££

I want to go here ☐

CLIMB ON A ROCK

...at Yelverton

Dartmoor is covered with rock. We don't mean the sugary pink stuff you get at the seaside. We're talking about big boulders. And if you know where to look, you can find rocks that are perfect for clambering over!

Yelverton is a village on the edge of Dartmoor. The area is pretty flat, but on Roborough Down, southwest of the town, there is a remarkable rock sticking out of the ground. It's the perfect playground for budding rock-climbers – just mind your step as you head to the top!

There's usually an ice-cream van parked next to the rock on summer days, so you can pick up refreshments once you've concluded your climbing. We think you'll agree that this place *rocks*!

Sticker Scores

5 ROCK-CLIMBER

4 HILL HIKER

3 RIVERSIDE RAMBLER

2 PAVEMENT WALKER

1 FELL OVER

Make A Day Of It

🔑 Play in a river. Head to nearby Magpie Bridge (also known as Bedford Bridge), where you can splash in a shallow river or run around on the grassy area beside the water.

🔑 Visit an ancient Abbey. Buckland Abbey used to be home to monks. Nowadays, you can try on a Tudor costume, run around in the meadows and orchards, or enjoy one of the woodland walks.

> ### Photo Op
> Climb to the top of the rock and get a snap of you standing on one leg at the summit!

← Yelverton's remarkable rock

Fascinating Facts

⭐ **During World War Two the area next to Yelverton Rock was used as an important airfield. The top floors of some houses were removed to make it easier for planes to land! Unfortunately this didn't stop the local church from being hit by an incoming plane. After the incident they put a red light on top of the church to prevent further collisions . . .**

⭐ Look out for the wartime bunkers that are still dotted around the former airfield. These were used to protect the soldiers from enemy attack.

> What is a mountaineer's favourite music?
> *Rock 'n' Roll!*

PLAN YOUR VISIT 23
Yelverton Rock
Roborough Down, Crapstone Road, PL20 6BT

`FREE`

I want to go here ☐

KEY

● Places

EAST DEVON

NORTH DEVON

SOUTH DEVON

CENTRAL CORNWALL

WEST CORNWALL

TOP FIVES

VISIT KING ARTHUR'S CASTLE

...at Tintagel Castle

Tintagel Castle is said to be the birthplace of King Arthur, the legendary British ruler. People disagree about whether he actually existed, but we can confirm that the castle's ruins are definitely real, and they're fit for a king!

The castle is perched on one of the most beautiful bits of Cornwall's rugged coast. It is accessible via a narrow bridge and steep steps – make your way down and imagine that you're at the centre of your own kingdom.

At low tide, you can also go down to Merlin's Cave, where King Arthur's magician advisor was supposed to have lived. But do be careful – the caves fill with water at high tide so check tide times before you visit.

Sticker Scores

5 – KING OF THE CASTLE

4 – BIG CASTLE

3 – RUINED CASTLE

2 – SAND CASTLE

1 – CHESS CASTLE

What was Camelot famous for?

Its *knight* life!

Make A Day Of It

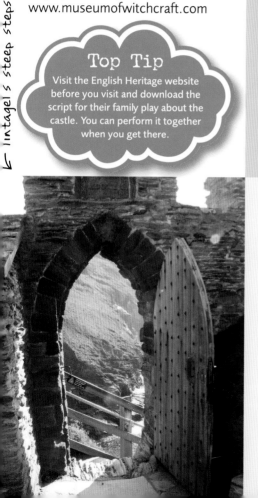

🔑 Wonder at a twenty-metre-high waterfall at nearby St Nectan's Glen. You'll also see a money tree, which has coins hammered into its trunk!

🔑 Get spooked at the Museum of Witchcraft in nearby Boscastle. It claims to have the world's largest display of witchy items. www.museumofwitchcraft.com

Top Tip

Visit the English Heritage website before you visit and download the script for their family play about the castle. You can perform it together when you get there.

Fascinating Facts

⭐ **King Arthur was famous for ruling the royal court of Camelot. Camelot had a round table, with no official seat for the most important person, because Arthur and all his knights were considered equals.**

⭐ King Arthur was also the owner of a sensational sword called Excalibur. It was given to him by The Lady of the Lake, a mysterious water-dwelling woman. Sadly, all we've ever found in our local lake is lots of mud and the occasional crisp packet . . .

Photo Op

Strike a royal pose in front of the ruins.

← Tintagel's steep steps

PLAN YOUR VISIT 24

Tintagel Castle
Tintagel, PL34 0HE
www.english-heritage.org.uk

📞 **01840 770328**

🕐 **Daily (peak) 10.00-18.00**
Daily (out of season) 10.00-16.00

£

I want to go here ☐

GO KARTING

...at St Eval Kart Circuit

Do you have a need for speed? A passion for pace? If so, get yourself to St Eval, where you'll be able to race proper petrol karts!

St Eval Kart Circuit is hidden just off the north Cornwall coast. There are three tremendous tracks: a ginormous one for grown-ups, a figure of eight for families and a tiny one for toddlers.

Sticker Scores

5 SPEEDY SUPER-CAR

4 CRACKING KART

3 REASONABLE RALLY CAR

2 STANDARD SALOON

1 CAR CRASH!

We love the family track, where, if you're aged six and over, you can race against adults! There are also three types of kart that all whizz along at super speeds. The cadet kart, for example (for kids aged between eight and eleven), has a top speed of twenty miles an hour! It's *Formula One*-derful!

Similar Spots

 Kartworld, near Liskeard, is run by the same people that own St Eval and also has cool karts for you to use.
www.kartworldcornwall.co.uk

 Coast 2 Coast Karting, near Hayle, has karts for kids aged eight and over, plus coin-operated karts for smaller speedsters.
www.chycor.co.uk/jeepers

 North Devon Karting has a junior kart club for regular visitors. They also offer brilliant birthday parties.
www.northdevonkarting.co.uk

Top Tip

Karting is not all about speed – you also need to know when to slow down. You'll complete a circuit faster if you work out how to brake as you approach a corner.

Fascinating Facts

★ The cadet karts are fitted with a 120 cubic centimetre (cc) Honda engine. That's twice as powerful as most small motorbikes! So remember to brake when you get to a bend . . .

Best Of The Rest

 See where candles are crafted. The St Eval Candle Company is based just round the corner from the karting circuit. Call ahead and they might arrange a tour for you!
www.stevalcandlecompany.co.uk

PLAN YOUR VISIT 25

St Eval Kart Circuit
St Eval, Wadebridge, PL27 7UN
www.cornwallkarting.com

 01637 860160

⊘ Opening hours vary throughout year

££ - £££

I want to go here ☐

CYCLE ON A CAMEL

...on the Camel Trail

Normally we wouldn't suggest you try cycling on a camel. They're too humpy and too hairy to make for a satisfying ride. Thankfully, the Camel Trail doesn't feature any actual camels – but it is one of the best cycle tracks in England!

The Camel Trail is the name for the stretch of disused railway line that runs between Padstow and Bodmin. Start your journey in Padstow, Wadebridge or Bodmin – there are bicycle hire points in each place. You'll pedal along pretty paths and through charming countryside. The full trail is eighteen miles long, but you don't have to cycle the whole thing. And if you want to share the workload, why not persuade a grown-up to join you on a tandem!

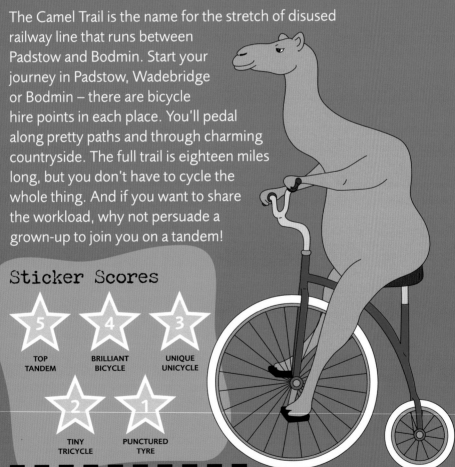

Sticker Scores

5 TOP TANDEM

4 BRILLIANT BICYCLE

3 UNIQUE UNICYCLE

2 TINY TRICYCLE

1 PUNCTURED TYRE

Make A Day Of It

🔑 View a vineyard at Camel Valley, just off the trail near Bodmin. It's one of the few places in the UK where wine is made. There's also a cool café on the side of a hill which is a good spot to take a pause during your journey.

Similar Spots

🔑 Check out the terrific Tarka Trail in Devon. It covers 30 miles between Braunton and Meeth, and is another brilliant place to go biking.

What is brown, has a hump and lives at the North Pole?

A lost camel!

Fascinating Facts

⭐ **The trail is named after the river Camel, which runs alongside it. However, no camels ever lived nearby – the name comes from an old Cornish word meaning 'crooked'.**

⭐ A camel is able to store energy in its humps, which means it can live without food in the desert for several months. Sadly, however, there is no food hidden along the Camel trail, so we suggest you pack a picnic!

Top Tip
Download the Camel Trail leaflet from the website before you visit. It includes a map and some top tips on where to go along the way.

PLAN YOUR VISIT 26

The Camel Trail
Padstow to Bodmin
www.cornwall.gov.uk

📞 0300 1234 100

FREE (using the trail)

££ (hiring a bicycle)

I want to go here ☐

← A bridge over the Camel Trail

LEARN TO SURF

...at Harlyn Surf School

Learning to surf is not easy, but once you've ridden a wave you'll think it's well worth the effort. So if you think surfing's cool then you need to get yourself to a surf school!

Harlyn Bay is one of North Cornwall's nicest beaches. It's also a good place to learn to surf as its waves are relatively gentle. Harlyn Surf School offers a range of lessons: you can choose anything from a one-off family session to a five-day summer camp.

Alternatively, you can leave the board behind and take one of the Surf School's coasteering sessions. This superb sport involves jumping off rocks, exploring caves and wading through rock pools. Whatever you choose, we're sure you won't get *board*!

Sticker Scores

5 SUPER SURF

4 WONDERFUL WAVE

3 REASONABLE RIPPLE

2 SHALLOW SEA

1 WAT-ER DISAPOINTMENT

Best Of The Rest

🔑 Walk out to a lighthouse. Harlyn bay is a 30-minute walk from Trevose Head Lighthouse. This impressive structure was built in 1847 and it still functions today, though it's been operated automatically since 1995.

Top Tip
Surfing and coasteering can both be dangerous without proper training and supervision, so we recommend you don't do either on your own.

← Surf's up!

Fascinating Facts

★ **The largest wave ever surfed was over 21 metres high! The man on the board was called Pete Cabrinha and the wave was in Hawaii. It sounds pretty dangerous to us – we're not sure *Haw-aii* did it!**

★ In 2005, 47 people managed to ride the same enormous surfboard in Snapper Rocks, Australia! Thankfully, at Harlyn Surf School they stick to one board per person . . .

How do you say hello to the sea?
Wave!

PLAN YOUR VISIT 27
Harlyn Surf School
Harlyn Bay, Nr Padstow, PL28 8SB
www.harlynsurfschool.co.uk
📞 01841 533 076
🕙 Daily (peak) 09.30 & 13.30
£££

I want to go here ☐

FISH FOR MACKEREL

...off Padstow Harbour

Fishing can be boring – you can sit by a river all day and not catch a thing. However, if you take a fishing trip from **Padstow** there's a very good chance you'll come back with a mound of mackerel!

Mackerel don't like to be near the shore, so the best fishing spots are usually only accessible by boat. The area a little out to sea from Padstow (past Hawker's Cove) is particularly popular.

Fishing trips run from Padstow Harbour most days during peak season. There are several operators – ask in the Padstow Angling Centre to learn who's heading out that week. Just check the weather forecast first to make sure it's not too choppy, or you might end up with an upset stomach!

Sticker Scores

★ 5 — **MASSIVE MACKEREL**

★ 4 — **HANDSOME HADDOCK**

★ 3 — **CRACKING COD**

★ 2 — **SMALL STICKLEBACK**

★ 1 — **SHARK ATTACK!**

Who's the head of the fish mafia?
The *cod*-father!

Similar Spots

🔑 A number of mackerel fishing boats run from Newquay Harbour – pop into the Newquay Harbour Boatmen's Association on South Quay Hill for more information. www.newquay-harbour.com

🔑 You can also fish for mackerel from Paignton Harbour – see www.mackerelfishing.co.uk for details.

Top Tip
Get the grown-ups to park in the car park above Padstow, on the junction of the A389 and New Street. It's next to a great playground, and it's also less busy than the jam-packed ones beside the harbour.

Fascinating Facts

⭐ **Cod is the most common fish used to make fish and chips, but it's also a threatened species because of overfishing. Increasingly chippies are using Pollock instead, because there are still plenty of them in our waters and it tastes just as good.**

⭐ Surprisingly, fish does not always need to be cod to be sold as cod! Haddock and whiting are both from the cod family and so shops are sometimes still allowed to call them cod.

⭐ **The world's largest freshwater fish is the catfish. One was caught in Thailand in 2005 which was around three metres long. That's taller than two eleven year olds standing on top of each other!**

PLAN YOUR VISIT 28

Padstow Angling Centre

1-3 S Quay, Padstow, PL28 8BL

📞 **01841 532 762**

🕐 **Call ahead to check tour times**

£££

I want to go here ☐

SPOT WILDLIFE

...in Cardinham Woods

Cornwall may be known for its brilliant beaches, but some of our favourite spots lie inland. And Cardinham is one place you *wood* be mad to miss!

Cardinham is a wonderful wood near Bodmin. Take one of the four marked trails through the trees – they're perfect for walking, cycling or horse riding.

While you're on your way, why not search for insects and dragonflies? Alternatively, see if you can spot some of the woods' shyer inhabitants – Cardinham is home to dormice, deer, buzzards, otters and kingfishers. Make sure you also leave time for a trip to the Woods Café. As well as having cracking cream teas and chompable chocolate cake, they also run fun activities such as den building and butterfly spotting.

Sticker Scores

⭐ **5** — FANTASTIC FOREST

⭐ **4** — WONDERFUL WOOD

⭐ **3** — DANK DINGLE

⭐ **2** — CREEPY COPSE

⭐ **1** — TREE STUMP

Photo Op

Hug a tree! Find your favourite and get a picture of you with your arms around its trunk.

Make A Day Of It

 Climb through caves at Carnglaze Caverns. There are three underground caverns with a shimmering subterranean lake. Oh, and they also have a dragon! www.carnglaze.com

 Visit some problem animals! Ever wondered where zoo animals go when they are badly behaved? Well, Porfell is the answer. You'll see obstinate ostriches, zany zebras and elderly meerkats! www.porfellanimalland.co.uk

← Cardinham Woods

> **Did you hear about the two silkworms that had a race?**
>
> It ended in a tie!

Fascinating Facts

★ **When trees get really ancient (over 400 years old) they start shrinking! They gradually get shorter and fatter, making them a better shape to cope with high winds and bad weather.**

★ The UK is one of the least wooded places in Europe. Only twelve per cent of the country is covered in woods and forest, compared over 30 per cent in much of Europe! However, we think the woods we do have (like Cardinham) are *tree*-mendous!

Similar Spots

 Haldon Forest Park, near Exeter, is another wicked woodland. It has den building, a play area, trails, rare butterflies and other wildlife. www.forestry.gov.uk/haldonforestpark

PLAN YOUR VISIT 29

Cardinham Woods
Cardinham, Nr. Bodmin, Cornwall
www.forestry.gov.uk/cardinham

📞 **01208 78111**

🕐 **Café open daily 10.30-16.30**

£ **(car park)** ✕

I want to go here ☐

RAMBLE THROUGH A RAINFOREST

...at the Eden Project

Cornwall may not be tropical, but that doesn't stop it from having its own rainforest. The incredible Eden Project is home to two dramatic domes, each with its own microclimate!

This amazing place contains peculiar plants and amazing animals from around the world. They live in biomes – ginormous greenhouses that look like bizarre bubbly mountains. One contains a Mediterranean landscape, while the other contains a re-created rainforest.

We particularly like the rainforest biome: you can see bananas growing on trees and walk around an indoor waterfall! Delve into the greenery or ride the rainforest balloon up to the top of the canopy (the bit among the tree tops). It's like a bit of Brazil has been plonked in the middle of Cornwall!

Sticker Scores

5 PERFECT PARADISE

4 GLORIOUS GARDEN

3 FANTASTIC FOREST

2 GRIMY GLADE

1 WOEFUL WOOD

Best Of The Rest

🔑 Admire Eden's amazing gardens. Over three-quarters of the Eden Project is outside. If you go in spring, look out for the Eden daffodil – a special species named after the project.

🔑 Build a den! In the summer the Eden Project lays on activities for kids, including den building and storytelling.

🔑 Skate around an ice rink. Eden usually erects an awesome ice rink over Christmas – check the website for details.

What flower grows right under your nose?
Two-lips!

← Eden's bizarre-looking biomes

Fascinating Facts

⭐ **The rainforest biome is a massive 240 metres long, 110 metres wide and 50 metres high. It's so big that you could fit about 15,000 London buses inside it!**

⭐ An area of rainforest the size of the Eden biome is destroyed on Earth every ten seconds. This is particularly worrying because the rainforest helps to slow down climate change.

Make A Day Of It

🔑 Stop off in the nearby Luxulyan valley. This beautiful steep-sloped area contains lots of Cornish mining remains.

PLAN YOUR VISIT 30

Eden Project
Bodelva, PL24 2SG
www.edenproject.com

📞 **01726 811 911**

🕐 **Daily (peak) 09.30-18.00**
Daily (out of season) 09.30-16.30
Late opening on selected summer evenings

£££

I want to go here ☐

GO BODYBOARDING

...at Watergate Bay

For those of you who don't fancy learning to surf standing up (see p68), here's an awesome alternative. At Watergate Bay you can hire a dramatic double bodyboard and ride a wave with someone beside you!

Watergate Bay is a terrific two-mile stretch of beach near Newquay. It's also home to the Extreme Academy, which describes itself as a ski resort on the beach. That doesn't mean there's snow everywhere – it's because they combine a hip hotel and cool café with cracking board sports.

Our favourite option is to hire a double bodyboard. You walk out into the waves with one other person, then cling onto the handles and launch yourselves into the waves. Hang on tight!

Sticker Scores

5 BODYBOARD

4 SURFBOARD

3 LONGBOARD

2 MALIBU BOARD

1 CARDBOARD

Best Of The Rest

 Learn to surf – the academy offers lessons for kids aged eight and over.

 Eat breakfast at Fifteen Cornwall. Just above Watergate Bay is a restaurant owned by Jamie Oliver, the famous TV chef. It's a great place for a meal at any time of day, but we think their breakfasts are a brilliant way to fill up before a busy day of beach fun.

Top Tip

If you'd rather watch the experts, check the Extreme Academy website for details of surfing competitions held at Watergate Bay. There are several impressive events held throughout the year.

Fascinating Facts

★ Bodyboarding is much easier than stand-up surfing. The boards are shorter and easier to carry, and the technique is easy to learn. Basically, you just lie on the board and cling to it while waves carry you into the water. We're *shore* you'll get the hang of it!

★ Cornwall has 165 beaches (and more if you count hidden coves)! So you could go to a different one each day for five and a half months!

Photo Op

Make sure somebody gets a snap of you catching a wave on your double bodyboard. Make your most fearless face!

← "Where have all the waves gone?"

PLAN YOUR VISIT 31

Extreme Academy
Watergate Bay, TR8 4AA
www.watergatebay.co.uk
☎ 01637 860 543
🕐 Opening hours vary throughout year
£ ☂

I want to go here ☐

RIDE A STEAM TRAIN

...at Lappa Valley Steam Railway

Most people look forward to an easy life when they retire, but not Eric Booth. Instead of relaxing, when Eric retired from the RAF he decided to follow his dream and construct a steam railway . . .

Lappa Valley was originally part of the main train line that ran from Newquay to Chacewater. Then, when it shut in 1963, it was bought by Eric, who turned it into a superb steam railway and activity park. You start your journey at Benny Halt station and then chug along at ten miles an hour until you get to East Wheal Rose. There's loads to do at the East Wheal Rose end of the line, from hiring boats to krazy golf. You'll *lappa* it up!

Sticker Scores

5 SUPER STEAM TRAIN

4 LARGE LOCOMOTIVE

3 CLASSY CHOO-CHOO

2 TRUNDLING TRAM

1 LEAVES ON THE LINE

Best Of The Rest

Walk around the brick maze at East Wheal Rose. Then, once you've completed it, stand back and look at its shape – it's designed to look like an original high-pressure steam engine.

Top Tip

Look at the locomotive as you travel. You'll see that the driver occasionally allows steam to escape, reducing pressure and power in the engine. This is why people sometimes say that someone running about is 'letting off steam'.

"All aboard!"

Fascinating Facts

★ **The first ever railway steam train was built by a Cornishman called Richard Trevithick.**

★ The UK used to have many more miles of railway than it does now. But in the 1960s a man called Dr Beeching, who was the chairman of British Railways, caused the closure of around 25 per cent of the network – a whopping 4,000 miles. That's enough train track to take you from Newquay to Chicago in the USA (though you might get wet along the way)!

★ **As well as being a station on the Lappa Valley line, East Wheal Rose is also the site of a terrible Cornish mining disaster. The mine here flooded in 1846 after a huge thunderstorm, killing 39 men and boys.**

PLAN YOUR VISIT 32

Lappa Valley Steam Railway
St Newlyn East, Newquay, TR8 5LX
www.lappavalley.co.uk

☎ **01872 510317**

🕐 **Daily (peak) 10.30-17.20**

££

I want to go here ☐

EXPLORE A LOST GARDEN

...at Heligan

Heligan really is a lost garden. One hundred years ago, it was one of the finest estates in England. However, during the last century everyone gradually forgot about these once grand gardens. Well, almost everyone . . .

Where am I ?

Thankfully, in 1990, two people called John Willis and Tim Smit gathered a group of enthusiasts and restored the gardens. It was a huge task which took six years, but thanks to their efforts Heligan is now one of the most popular gardens in the UK.

Heligan covers 200 acres, with each section based on a different theme. You can visit the Victorian Gardens, see giant rhubarb in the Jungle, or admire animals in the Wildlife Project. You'll be glad the gardens of Heligan are well again!

Sticker Scores

5 — LOST GARDEN

4 — HANGING GARDEN

3 — ROSE GARDEN

2 — VEGETABLE GARDEN

1 — COMPOST HEAP

Top Tip

During the summer, Heligan holds night-time bat walks! A bat expert guides you on an adventure, teaching you how to identify the calls of British bats.

Make A Day Of It

Spot rare birds at nearby Wingz Bird Sanctuary. This place protects and breeds rare and endangered birds. www.wingzbirdsanctuary.co.uk

Visit a tortoise garden! If you're tired of trees and fed up of flowers, head to this tortoise sanctuary. They have over 140 tortoises, from babies to the over 90s! www.thetortoisegarden.co.uk

Discover how china is made. Wheal Martyn Industrial Museum is a working china pit combined with a country park and wonderful woodland walks. There's also a challenge trail and a play area for kids. www.wheal-martyn.com

Why do potatoes make good detectives?
They keep their eyes *peeled*!

Fascinating Facts

★ Heligan is home to a pineapple pit – a clever place for growing pineapples in cooler climates. Usually these fruits only grow in much hotter countries. However, at Heligan the pit is kept warm during the winter months using a mixture of tree bark and horse poo!

★ One of the Seven Wonders of the Ancient World was a gorgeous garden known as the Hanging Gardens of Babylon. The gardens were supposedly destroyed around 2,000 years ago and some people question whether they ever actually existed. We're just glad Heligan didn't suffer the same fate!

PLAN YOUR VISIT 33

Lost Gardens of Heligan
Pentewan, St.Austell, PL26 6EN
www.heligan.com

📞 01726 845100

🕐 Daily (peak) 10.00-18.00
Daily (out of season) 10.00-17.00

££

I want to go here ☐

MILK A COW

...at Dairyland Farm World

In the old days you milked a cow by sitting on a stool and pulling its udders. These days, things are much more high tech, with multiple cows attached to pipes, tubes and bottles. And it's *udder*-ly fascinating to watch!

Dairyland is a cow-themed farm park, but there's plenty to see and do that doesn't *moo*! You can bottle-feed baby animals, ride a pony, zoom down a drop slide and even ride a Lamborghini tractor!

However, our favourite bits are all cow-related. We suggest you start your visit by having a go at milking Dairyland's life-size plastic cow, then go and see real cows being milked in the massive milking parlour. You're guaranteed to *heifer* good time!

Sticker Scores

5 CRACKING COW	4 HAPPY HEIFER	3 BIG BULL
2 LAZY LIVESTOCK	1 MINCED BEEF	

What do you get when you sit under a cow?
A pat on the head!

Make A Day Of It

🔑 Slide down a chute at nearby Oasis Hendra swimming park, where you'll find all kinds of indoor and outdoor watery attractions. www.oasis-hendra.co.uk

Similar Spots

🔑 Pennywell Farm, near Totnes in Devon, has fantastic rides plus plenty of ponies, pigs and other animals. www.pennywellfarm.co.uk

🔑 Featherdown is a fantastic network of real working farms across the UK. Visitors can stay on one for a few days and help the farmers out with their daily tasks. www.featherdownfarm.co.uk

Fascinating Facts

⭐ **Cows have four stomachs! Grass is hard to digest, so it needs to pass through several different parts of the cow to be properly digested.**

⭐ Each cow has a unique pattern on its coat – so no two are ever the same. Think of it as the cow version of fingerprints!

⭐ **The proper name for a group of cows is cattle. Cows are the female ones, whereas males are called bulls. Young cattle are known as calves, and young females who have not had their own calves are heifers. So working out what to call them is quite *cow*-plicated!**

← What are you staring at?

PLAN YOUR VISIT 34

DairyLand Farmworld
Nr Newquay, TR8 5AA
www.dairylandfarmworld.com

📞 **01872 510246**

🕐 **Daily (peak) 10.00-17.00**

I want to go here ☐

EAT FISH AND CHIPS IN A HARBOUR

...in Padstow

We're not big fans of posh nosh. Give us a choice of fancy food or fish and chips and we'll take the fish and chips every time. And if we can eat them beside some boats . . . well, we can't think of anything *batter*!

> What is a sea monster's favourite supper?
>
> Fish 'n' ships!

Padstow is a pretty fishing town that's home to several seafood spots owned by a famous chef called Rick Stein. We particularly like his fish and chip shop on South Quay. It has a restaurant attached, but we suggest you pick up a takeaway and head for the harbour. Walk along the waterfront, past the herring boats and lobster catchers, until you get to the main seating area. Just be careful the seagulls don't steal your supper!

Sticker Scores

5 — CHIPS
4 — ROAST POTATOES
3 — MASH
2 — BOILED POTATOES
1 — RAW POTATOES

Make A Day Of It

🔑 Play crazy golf on the side of a hill. Greens Café on North Quay has a cool crazy-golf course and café with great views of the harbour.

🔑 Go crabbing. The harbour is the perfect place to catch these little critters (see p70).

🔑 Learn about lobsters at the National Lobster Hatchery. You'll find out how they shed their skins, and if you really fall for them you can even adopt your own!

🔑 Fish for mackerel. Daily fishing trips run from Padstow harbor – ask at the tourist office for details.

Similar Spots

⭐ If you're in south Cornwall, you can still sample Rick Stein's fish and chips – at his second shop in Falmouth. And don't worry if you can't get to one of Stein's spots – there are cracking chippies all throughout the region!

Top Tip

Hang around Padstow's harbour during the summer months and there's a good chance you'll hear a brass band. Groups from all around the county perform regular quayside concerts from May to September.

↙ Fantastic fish and chips

PLAN YOUR VISIT ③⑤

Stein's Fish & Chips
South Quay, Padstow, PL28 8BL
www.rickstein.com
📞 01841 532700
🕐 Daily 11.30-21.00
££

I want to go here ☐

PICK YOUR OWN FRUIT

...at Pencarrow House and Gardens

We love strawberries and raspberries, and they never taste better then when you pick them yourself!

Pencarrow House is a stunning stately home with grand gardens. But don't fear – this isn't the sort of place where they tell you off for running on the grass. In fact, they actively encourage it! There's a fabulous hill to roll down, a cool children's play area with a Wendy house, and proud peacocks roaming around.

We particularly like the pick–your-own part of Pencarrow. You can stock up on strawberries, rummage for raspberries and go hunting for gooseberries. Take them home and make them into jam, or just scoff them fresh from the punnet. Just make sure you've paid for them first!

Sticker Scores

5 — STRAWBERRY PICKER

4 — GOOSEBERRY PICKER

3 — BLUEBERRY PICKER

2 — RASPBERRY PICKER

1 — NOSE PICKER

Similar Spots

There are plenty of places to pick your own fruit in the region. For a full list go to www.pickyourownfarms.org.uk Here are a few of our favourites:

🔑 Trevaskis Farm, near Hayle, has a huge selection of pick-your-own fruit and veg.
www.trevaskisfarm.co.uk

🔑 Lifton Strawberry Fields is a Devon delight that unsurprisingly specialises in succulent strawberries!
www.liftonstrawberryfields.co.uk

🔑 Chyreen Fruit Farm is just south of Truro. You can pick tempting treats such as strawberries, gooseberries, blackcurrants and redcurrants. www.chyreen.ukf.net

Berry nice indeed!

Fascinating Facts

⭐ **A curious species of tree known as the monkey puzzle got its name at Pencarrow. A lawyer called Charles Austin was staying at the house in 1834. When he saw the tree's strange, symmetrical branches he apparently said that it 'would puzzle a monkey'.**

⭐ Pencarrow is on the edge of Bodmin Moor, which is said to be home to a colossal creature called the Beast of Bodmin. People say it's a bit like a huge lion, but we think they're *lyin'*!

Photo Op
See if you can get a pic of a peacock displaying its colourful tail.

PLAN YOUR VISIT 36
Pencarrow House and Gardens
Bodmin, Cornwall, PL30 3AG
www.pencarrow.co.uk

📞 **01208 841369**

🕐 **Gardens: daily (peak) 09.30-17.30 Check website for house opening times**

I want to go here ☐

RIDE A PONY

...at Springfields Fun Park and Pony Centre

We like Springfields because there's so much to do – as well as equine entertainment, there's also boating, karting and all kinds of cuddly creatures. It's the perfect place to *horse* around for the day!

The *mane* attraction, of course, is the Pony Centre. You can stroke and groom these adorable animals, watch them perform in the daily pony show, then ride one yourself. Choose anything from a quick circuit of the pony track to a trek through the woods.

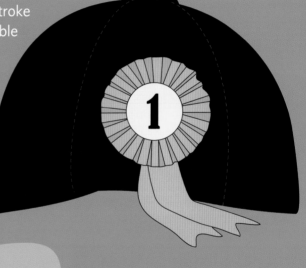

Sticker Scores

★ 5 — HAPPY HORSE

★ 4 — PRANCING PONY

★ 3 — SUPREME STALLION

★ 2 — FANTASTIC FOAL

★ 1 — DEPRESSED DONKEY

Once you've trotted about on a pony you can feed the fish, stroke pets, or race the pedal karts. And if the weather's bad you can always head to the indoor playground, which has a death drop and wave slides. It's our number one fun park!

Fascinating Facts

⭐ You can tell how old a horse is by looking at its teeth. This is because unlike humans, horses' teeth keep growing throughout their lives. That's why old people are sometimes described as 'Long in the tooth'.

⭐ Horses are able to sleep standing up without falling over! They have special tendons in their legs that help them to support their weight for a long time.

⭐ Horses can see things behind them! Unlike humans, their eyes are located on the sides of their heads, so they have a view backwards. So don't pull a rude face behind their back, or you might end up with a moany pony!

⊢ Getting ready to ride a pony

Top Tip
Check the website before you visit – there are often discounts available for online ticket purchases.

A horse walks into a shop and says he's having a brilliant day.
The shopkeeper asks, 'So why the long face?'!

PLAN YOUR VISIT 37
Springfields Fun Park and Pony Centre
St Columb Major, Newquay, TR9 6HU
www.springfieldsponycentre.co.uk
📞 01637 881224
🕐 Daily (peak) 10.00-18.00

££

I want to go here ☐

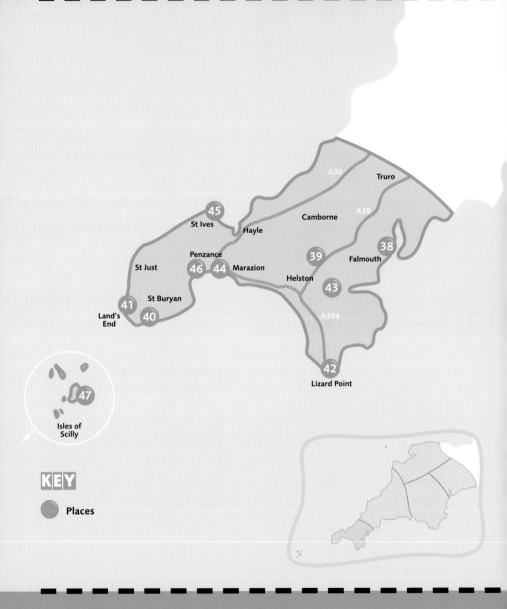

St Ives — 45

Hayle

Camborne

A30

Truro

A39

Falmouth — 38

Penzance

39

St Just

46 44 Marazion

Helston

43

St Buryan

A394

41 Land's End

40

42

Lizard Point

47

Isles of Scilly

KEY

● Places

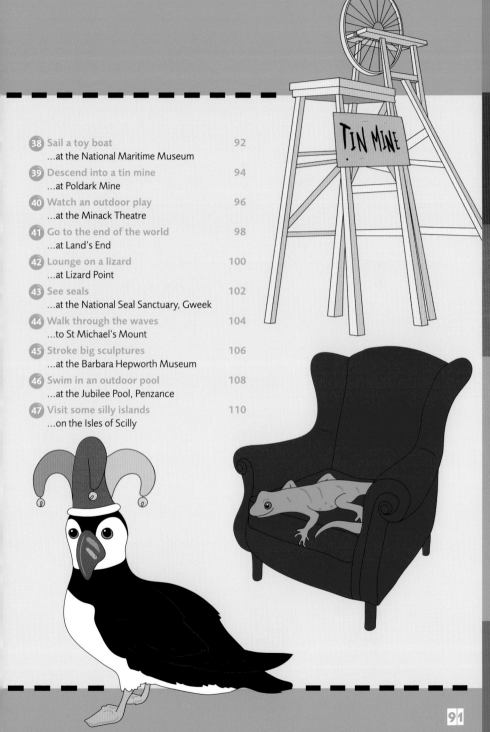

EAST DEVON

NORTH DEVON

SOUTH DEVON

CENTRAL CORNWALL

WEST CORNWALL

TOP FIVES

TIN MINE

SAIL A TOY BOAT

...at the National Maritime Museum

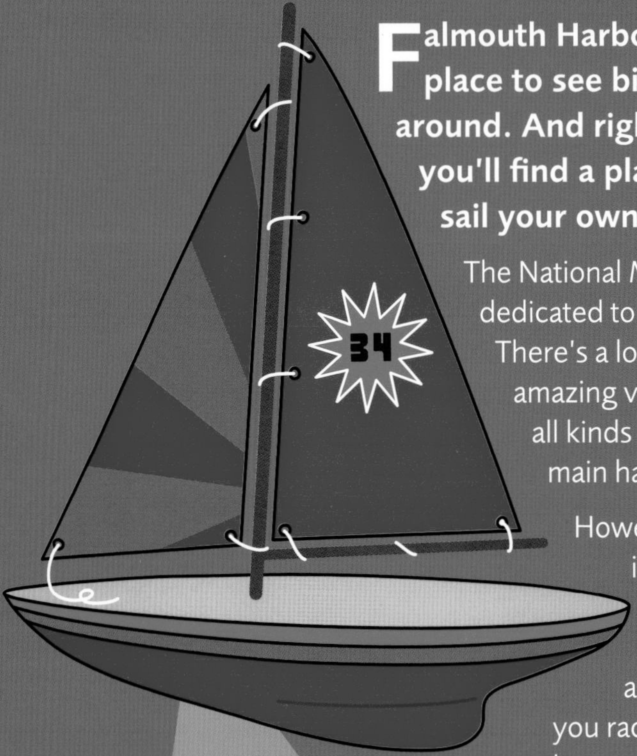

Falmouth Harbour is a brilliant place to see big boats bobbing around. And right on the waterfront you'll find a place where you can sail your own ship!

The National Maritime Museum is dedicated to all things shipshape. There's a lookout tower with amazing views over the docks and all kinds of model boats in the main hall.

However, our favourite part is the pool where you can sail toy yachts. Special fans blow wind across the water while you race your radio-controlled boat around a course. And once you've finished, you can walk out onto the pontoon and see real life-sized boats on the water. You'll have the *mari*-time of your life!

34

Sticker Scores

5 SHIPSHAPE

4 LOVELY LINER

3 BRILLIANT BOAT

2 USEFUL YACHT

1 SHIPWRECKED

What part of a fish weighs the most?

Its scales!

Make A Day Of It

🔑 **Splash around** in the nearby Ships and Castles fun pool. It's got a whooshing river, a wave machine and a shallow beach area. www.shipsandcastles.co.uk

🔑 **Be amazed by a laurel maze.** The maze at Glendurgan Garden was planted in 1833! www.nationaltrust.org.uk

🔑 **Go bowling.** Ocean Bowl has lanes, pool tables and video games. www.oceanbowl.co.uk

🔑 **Sing a seafarer's song** at the International Sea Shanty Festival, which takes place in Falmouth in June. Shanties are songs sung by sailors.

My boat's faster than your boat! ↙

Fascinating Facts

⭐ **In 1972 a shipwrecked family of six survived for a whopping 38 days in a tiny dinghy! The lifesaving vessel was called the Ednamair and it's on display in the Maritime Museum's Survival Zone.**

Best Of The Rest

🔑 **See under the sea!** Look into the harbour through large underwater windows in the Tidal Zone. You can see fish, shrimps, crabs and even birds diving down beneath the waves to find some lunch.

🔑 **Steer a ship through a narrow channel** in the interactive area.

PLAN YOUR VISIT 38

National Maritime Museum Cornwall
Discovery Quay, Falmouth, TR11 3QY
www.nmmc.co.uk

📞 01326 313 388

🕐 Daily 10.00-17.00

££

I want to go here ☐

DESCEND INTO A TIN MINE

...at Poldark Mine

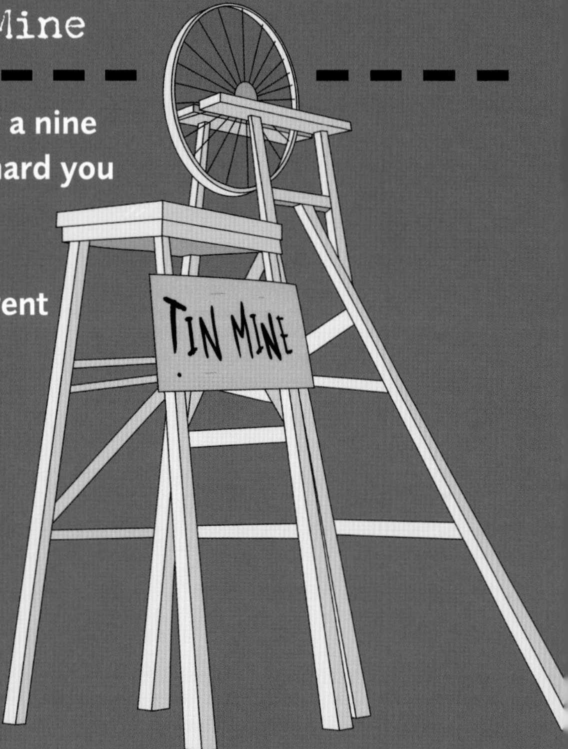

These days, if you say a nine year old is working hard you might imagine them in a maths lesson. However, things were rather different in the 1700s – kids of this age often worked in Cornwall's mines . . .

Poldark was an operational tin mine from around 1710 until 1790. Working there was tough stuff; boys loaded rocks into wheelbarrows underground, while the girls stayed on the surface breaking them up into smaller pieces.

When you visit, you'll take a guided tour of the tiny tunnels – some are less than 150 centimetres high. Keep an eye out for the narrow ladders and wet paths, which are signs of the terrible conditions that boys worked in. After this, maths lessons will seem like luxury!

Sticker Scores

5 CRISP TASTER

4 FOOTBALLER

3 POP STAR

2 OFFICE WORKER

1 TIN MINER

Best Of The Rest

🔑 **Play chess** on Poldark's giant chessboard.

🔑 **Paint your own pot** in the ceramics section of the site.

Top Tip
Take along a postcard to send from Poldark's postbox. It's deeper underground than any other in the country! Poldark also has its own special stamps.

Photo Op
Get a snap of you crouching in a tiny tin-mine tunnel.

← What does this plunger do?

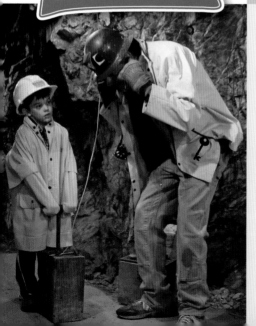

Fascinating Facts

⭐ **The most famous Cornish food, the pasty, started life as lunch for tin miners. This pastry pie was thrown down the mines to hungry workers below. They would munch on the meat inside then discard the dirty pastry.**

⭐ Hard rock mining started in Cornwall, and the miners of the county exported more than just their skills around the world. Plenty of countries still serve variations of pasty recipes that were introduced by visiting Cornishmen. In fact, it is said that more pasties are made in Mexico every year than are churned out in Cornwall!

⭐ **Couples can get married underground at Poldark! Your tour will pass through Holman's Chamber, which is licensed to hold wedding ceremonies.**

PLAN YOUR VISIT 39

Poldark Mine
Wendron, Helston, TR13 0ES
www.poldark-mine.co.uk
📞 **01326 573 173**
🕐 **Daily 10.00-17.30
(closed some Saturdays)**

££

I want to go here ☐

WATCH AN OUTDOOR PLAY

...at the Minack Theatre

Most theatres are indoors for a good reason – you wouldn't want to be sitting outside for very long on a chilly December evening! But if the weather's nice, the Minack offers a spectacular way to spend a few hours . . .

Perched precariously on the edge of a cliff, the Minack Theatre is carved into the rocks. They run a seventeen week summer season that includes pleasant plays, marvellous musicals and delightful dance. During August there are also special kids' shows.

Even if you don't see a show, this breathtaking place is worth a visit. Walk amongst the theatre seats, snack on a cream tea from the coffee shop, then stroll through the Minack's gorgeous gardens. The view is almost as dramatic as the acting!

Sticker Scores

5 — PERFECT PLAY

4 — BRILLIANT BALLET

3 — MEDIOCRE MIME

2 — STANDARD SHOW

1 — PLAY THE FOOL

Similar Spots

🔑 The Landmark in Ilfracombe is another theatre with a dramatic location. The building looks like two large upside-down buckets that have been plonked on the cliff edge, with the waves crashing behind them. Children's plays are performed in the summer. www.northdevontheatres.org

Top Tip

Take a hat and sun cream for daytime shows, and wrap up warm if you're visiting in the evening. Also, if you don't want a sore bum, hire a cushion at the venue (or remember to bring your own)!

Fascinating Facts

⭐ The Minack Theatre looks like a Roman creation, but it was actually built during the 1900s by a remarkable woman called Rowena Cade. The first performance took place in 1932 with the stage partly lit by car headlights!

⭐ Rowena never received enough money from the plays to fund the theatre – so she paid for much of the construction work from her own pocket.

⭐ Minack means 'rocky place' in Cornish. That's a pretty good description of these impressive cliffs!

What happens when a ghost haunts a theatre?
The actors get stage fright!

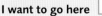

PLAN YOUR VISIT 40

The Minack Theatre & Visitor Centre

Porthcurno, Penzance, TR19 6JU

www.minack.com

📞 01736 810181

🕐 Thu & Sat-Tue (peak) 09.30-17.00
Wed & Fri (peak) 09.30-12.00
Daily (out of season) 10.00-15.30

£ (visiting only)

£££ (performances)

I want to go here ☐

← Minack Theatre

GO TO THE END OF THE WORLD

...at Land's End

OK, so this might not be the end of the world, but it is the end point of the UK. Land's End is the most southwesterly point of the British mainland – and there's a sign to prove it!

Land's End is popular because of its position – people often cycle between here and John o'Groats, in Scotland, at the top of the country. There's plenty to do here – you can choose from a range of visitor attractions or alternatively take a walk along the wind-swept cliffs. While you're walking, look out for dolphins, porpoises and basking sharks. Whatever you do, just don't forget to stop at the car park, because if you carry on you'll run out of road!

!

World ends ahead

Sticker Scores

5 WORLD'S END   4 LAND'S END   3 CITY LIMITS

2 CUL-DE-SAC   1 DEAD END

Make A Day Of It

🔑 Feed animals at Greeb Farm, just a short walk from the Land's End car park.

🔑 Build a sandcastle on nearby Sennen Beach. This is a relatively quiet spot, with white sand that's perfect for creating castles.

🔑 Hunt for a shipwreck at Mayon Cliff near Sennen Cove. RMS *Mulheim* washed up here in 2003 and can still be seen from the path above.

Fascinating Facts

⭐ In 1968, the *Torrey Canyon* supertanker crashed into the Cornish coast between Land's End and the Scilly Isles. It spilled 31 million gallons of oil into the sea, causing an environmental disaster. Eventually it was bombed by the RAF to help break it up and set alight to the oil.

⭐ John o'Groats and Land's End are 603 miles apart. However, it takes at least 838 miles to travel between the two by road – so it's quite a trek for those who choose to make the journey!

Photo Op

Get a snap of you next to the famous Land's End signpost. For a fee you can choose to have a photo taken with the sign altered to point to your home town!

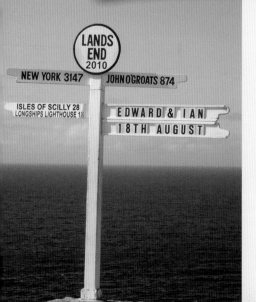

PLAN YOUR VISIT 41

Land's End
Sennen, TR19 7AA
www.landsend-landmark.co.uk

📞 0871 720 0044

🕐 Daily (summer) 10.00-17.00
Daily (off peak) 10.30-15.30
Late opening on selected August evenings

£ (parking)   ££ (attractions and parking)

🍴 🎁 ☂

I want to go here ☐

LOUNGE ON A LIZARD

...at Lizard Point

OK, so we're not actually suggesting you lie on a green reptile! This particular lizard is, in fact, the southernmost part of the UK.

The Lizard is the part of Cornwall that looks like the heel of a boot. Lizard Point is its southern tip, and a beautiful place for a country walk beside steep cliffs and crashing waves.

Park at Lizard Point and walk to Kynance Cove – the round trip is just under five miles long. You'll see the Lizard lighthouse, the old lifeboat station and plenty of hidden coves. Look out for the Cornish chough – a crow which became extinct in the county but has now returned. The locals must be *choughed* to bits!

Sticker Scores

☆ 5	☆ 4	☆ 3
LARGE LIZARD	GINORMOUS GECKO	COLOSSAL CHAMELEON

☆ 2	☆ 1
SIZEABLE SALAMANDER	LARGE BLIZZARD

Make A Day Of It

Polish off a perfect pasty! **Head to the Lizard Pasty Shop in Lizard village. It's run by a remarkable woman called Ann Muller, who serves some of the best parcels of Cornish pastry we've ever tasted!** www.annspasties.co.uk

Enjoy ice cream **at Roskilly's ice-cream farm in St Keverne. You'll see cows being milked and learn how fresh Cornish cream gets turned into the icy stuff.** www.roskillys.co.uk

Fascinating Facts

★ **The Lizard has its very own rock! Serpentine is a dark green stone which is unique to the Lizard. Red and white lines run through it, and it's used by local craftspeople to make ornaments and jewellery.**

★ The Cornish chough has a red bill and a black body. Though the birds disappeared from Cornwall in 1973, they've now returned to the Lizard and Penwith with the help of the Royal Society for the Protection of Birds (RSPB). Look out for them on shops, signs and posters throughout the county.

Photo Op

Lizard Point can be a spectacular spot to see curiously shaped clouds. Why not take a photo of your favourite and upload it onto the website of the Cloud Appreciation Society? www.cloudappreciationsociety.org

PLAN YOUR VISIT 42

Lizard Point
Nr Helston, TR12
www.nationaltrust.org.uk
 01326 561407
FREE NT

I want to go here ☐

WEST CORNWALL

SEE SEALS

...at the National Seal Sanctuary, Gweek

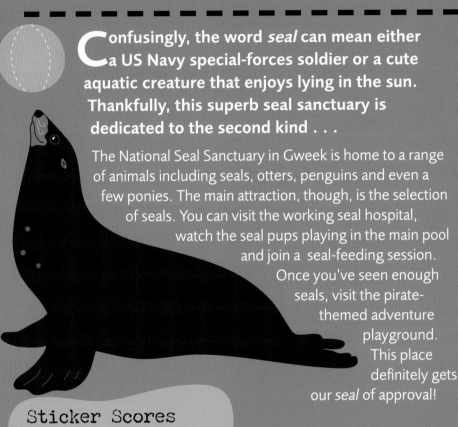

Confusingly, the word *seal* can mean either a US Navy special-forces soldier or a cute aquatic creature that enjoys lying in the sun. Thankfully, this superb seal sanctuary is dedicated to the second kind . . .

The National Seal Sanctuary in Gweek is home to a range of animals including seals, otters, penguins and even a few ponies. The main attraction, though, is the selection of seals. You can visit the working seal hospital, watch the seal pups playing in the main pool and join a seal-feeding session. Once you've seen enough seals, visit the pirate-themed adventure playground. This place definitely gets our *seal* of approval!

Sticker Scores

5 SUPERB SEAL

4 WONDERFUL WALRUS

3 IMPRESSIVE PENGUIN

2 STANDARD SEA-LION

1 *OTTER*-LY BORING

What do you call a seal that tells fibs?

Sea *lyin'*!

Best Of The Rest

← A suspicious-looking seal

🔑 Peer at penguins. Check out the colony of Humboldt penguins that live just next to the play area.

🔑 Touch crabs and starfish at the Rock Pool Experience, which runs during peak season.

🔑 Spot partially sighted seals. Look out for Ray, who is cross-eyed, and Babyface, who only has one eye!

Photo Op

Get a snap of a posing penguin – catch them on a good day and they'll sometimes perform for pictures!

Fascinating Facts

⭐ There are 33 different seal species in the world. The smallest is the Galapagos seal, which weighs around 30 kilogrammes. The largest – the southern bull elephant seal – can weigh a whopping two tonnes. That's the same size as a large car!

⭐ Seals communicate with each other by slapping the water and grunting. Not that we can understand what they're saying – it's all *Gweek* to us!

⭐ SEALs are the elite forces of the US Navy. In this case, SEAL stands for SEa Air and Land. Sadly, no actual seals assist with their operations.

PLAN YOUR VISIT 43

National Seal Sanctuary
Gweek, Near Helston, TR12 6UG
www.sealsanctuary.co.uk
📞 0871 423 2110
🕐 Opens daily at 10.00
Closing times vary

££

I want to go here ☐

WALK THROUGH THE WAVES

...to St Michael's Mount

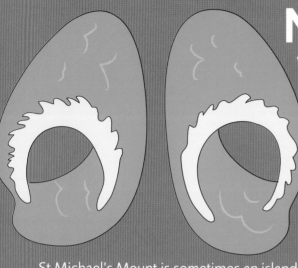

Normally we wouldn't recommend wandering through water. You're likely to get soggy, and there's always the risk of drowning. But at St Michael's Mount you can walk through the waves without getting wet!

St Michael's Mount is sometimes an island and sometimes part of the Cornish coast – it depends on the time of day! It is connected to the mainland by a causeway which you can walk along when the tide is low. It's like the waves have parted just for you!

Once you get to the island, check out the cool castle. We particularly like its gory defensive features – see if you can find the murdering hole (a gap through which soldiers could attack their enemies) and the guns between the turrets.

Sticker Scores

5	4	3
MASSIVE MOUNT	HUGE HILL	STANDARD SLOPE
2	1	
BORING BUMP	MEASLY MOUND	

Top Tip

Try a Cornish pasty at the Phillips bakery in Marazion. Just don't munch it on the boat, unless you want to get seasick!

Make A Day Of It

Take a boat to the mount. When the tide is high, we definitely don't suggest you try to walk through the waves! Instead, take the boat from one of the landing points on Marazion beach.

Play on the mile-long beach at Marazion, on the mainland.

Look for birds, dragonflies and rabbits at nearby Marazion Marsh, a free nature reserve.

Forage for food. Rachel Lambert runs wild-food walks from Marazion during the summer (see p123). www.wildwalks-southwest.co.uk

Fascinating Facts

★ **2,000 years ago, St Michael's Mount was an important port. Then it became a popular destination for religious pilgrims, before becoming a fortress in the Middle Ages.**

★ These days the mount is home to the St Aubyn family. They've lived there since 1647 and plan to stick around for a while. Although they gave the mount to the National Trust in 1954, the agreement allows them to live there for the next 999 years!

★ **St Michael's Mount is named after the Archangel Michael, who apparently appeared to fisherman there . . . But we think there's something *fishy* about that story!**

PLAN YOUR VISIT 44

St Michael's Mount
www.stmichaelsmount.co.uk
www.marazion.co.uk for causeway timings

📞 **01736 710507**

🕐 **Sun-Fri: causeway and ferry times vary**

FREE (walking) **£** (boat)
£ (castle)

I want to go here ☐

St Michael's Mount

WEST CORNWALL

STROKE BIG SCULPTURES

...at the Barbara Hepworth Museum

Most galleries tell you not to touch the exhibits in case you damage them. However, here you're actively encouraged to stroke the sculptures!
Now that's our kind of art . . .

St Ives is well-known for being home to lots of artists. One of the most famous was Barbara Hepworth, a sculptor who created natural-looking sculptures from stone, wood and bronze.

The studio and gardens where Barbara worked have now been turned into a museum. Our favourite part is the garden – you can stroll between the shrubs and get up close to the curiously curvy creations. Many of them have holes in the middle – we think they look like a cross between sculpture and Swiss cheese!

Sticker Scores

★ 5 — SMASHING SCULPTURE

★ 4 — VALUABLE VASE

★ 3 — SMALL STATUE

★ 2 — MODEST MODEL

★ 1 — SMASHED SCULPTURE

Photo Op
Get a snap of you peering through one of the many head-sized holes in Hepworth's sculptures!

Make A Day Of It

🔑 Admire modern art at Tate St Ives. This impressive gallery also owns the Hepworth Museum and often lays on activities for kids.

🔑 Walk to St Ives Island. This place is actually more of a peninsula than an island, but it does have great views. You can sometimes see dolphins, porpoises and rare birds.

🔑 Have your photo taken with a penguin! As well as penguins, Paradise Park, an animal sanctuary, has plenty of other creatures and an impressive play area.
www.paradisepark.org.uk

Fascinating Facts

⭐ **The most expensive British sculpture ever was made by Henry Moore, who was one of Barbara Hepworth's friends. It sold for £3.7 million in 2003. That's not a bad price for three lumps of bronze!**

⭐ The smallest sculptures in the world are so tiny they are only visible through a microscope! The mini-marvels are by British sculptor Willard Wigan and include a model of an astronaut and the Incredible Hulk.

Top Tip

Why not make your own sculpture on the beach? Or visit kids.tate.org.uk for details of how to create your own Hepworth masterpiece from a bar of soap!

← A curvy Hepworth sculpture

 **PLAN YOUR VISIT** 45

Barbara Hepworth Museum
Barnoon Hill, St Ives, TR26 1AD
www.tate.org.uk/stives

📞 01736 796 226

🕐 Daily (peak) 10.00-17.20
   Daily (out of season) 10.00-16.20

£ 🍴 🎁 ☂

I want to go here ☐

SWIM IN AN OUTDOOR POOL

...at the Jubilee Pool, Penzance

In the 1930s, outdoor swimming pools were all the rage. Most of these summer sunbathing spots – known as lidos – have closed down. But Penzance's impressive pool is still standing . . .

The gigantic Jubilee Pool opened in 1935 to mark King George's Silver Jubilee. At 100 metres long, it's one of the biggest pools in the country and its seaside location puts it amongst the prettiest too.

Sticker Scores

FRONT CRAWL

BREASTSTROKE

BACKSTROKE

DOGGY PADDLE   **ARM BANDS**

Why not head for a dip, then wander among the rock pools next to the Jubilee when you're finished? The pool also has a great café attached to it, which is perfect if you're peckish after a bit of breaststroke!

Make A Day Of It

🔑 Admire the boats in Penzance Harbour. You'll find a remarkable range of fishing and sailing boats bobbing about, just a short walk from the pool.

🔑 Go underground at Geevor Tin Mine. Unlike Poldark (see p94), which shut in the 1700s, Geevor stayed open until 1990! Take a tour and see what life was life for miners here.

Photo Op

Get a snap of St Michael's Mount, which is just east of Penzance. There are great views from the Jubilee Pool.

← Penzance's cool pool

Fascinating Facts

⭐ **Penzance was a target for pirates from the 1500s until the 1700s. Thankfully, you won't find Blackbeard or any other unpleasant pirate-types hanging out at the Jubilee Pool!**

⭐ Until a few hundred years ago, Cornwall had its own language. Penzance was one of the last places to stop speaking Cornish and adopt English instead. The last person known to have spoken only Cornish was Chesten Marchant. He died in 1676 in Gwithian, a few miles from Penzance.

> **What do you get when you cross a fish with an elephant?**
> *Swimming trunks!*

PLAN YOUR VISIT 46

Jubilee Pool

The Promenade, Penzance, TR18 4AA

www.jubileepool.co.uk

📞 01736 369 224

🕐 Daily (summer) 10.30-18.00

£

I want to go here ☐

VISIT SOME SILLY ISLANDS

...on the Isles of Scilly

These islands might have a *scilly* name, but they're still a great place for a break. In fact, we like them so much we think they should be renamed the Isles of Awesome!

The Isles of Scilly lie 30 miles off the Cornish coast. You can get there by helicopter, boat or plane – and once there you won't be short of things to do. Why not sample sea sports like sailing and kayaking, or hire a bike and explore the isles?

We like taking a boat between the isles – look out for Hangman Island, which was once supposedly a site for executions, and the now uninhabited island of Samson, where people used to survive on a diet of limpets and potatoes. Now that is *scilly*!

Sticker Scores

5 SCILLY ISLANDS	**4** AWESOME ARCHIPELAGO	**3** PERFECT PENINSULA
	2 REASONABLE ROCK	**1** SILLY ISLANDS

How do you describe a black-and-white bird that's out of breath?

Puffin'!

Best Of The Rest

🔑 Go crabbing (see p44) on St Mary's Pier.

🔑 Search for beads on St Agnes, one of the smaller islands. In the seventeenth century, a shipwreck spilled millions of beads onto the shore at Beady Pool here. Apparently if you look hard enough you can still spot washed-up beads on the beach – though we've yet to find one!

Top Tip

Keep an eye out for puffins while you're travelling around the Scillies. These cute black-and-white birds have big beaks and build nests on the outer islands.

Fascinating Facts

★ The Scilly Isles are home to a number of pilot gigs – Cornish six-seater boats. They were once used as lifeboats, but these days they are mostly for sport. The Scilly Isles hosts the annual World Pilot Gig Championships (though we suspect most of the contestants come from Cornwall)!

★ Until about 1,500 years ago, the Scilly Isles were probably all part of one larger island. However, rising sea levels have caused them to be divided into 145 mini-islands.

PLAN YOUR VISIT 47

The Isles of Scilly
www.simplyscilly.co.uk
📞 01720 424031

I want to go here ☐

← Puffins on the Isles of Scilly

WEST CORNWALL

EAST DEVON

NORTH DEVON

SOUTH DEVON

CENTRAL CORNWALL

WEST CORNWALL

TOP FIVES

TOP FIVE

...things to spot

Devon and Cornwall are full of interesting things to spot. See how many of these you can identify!

Wild Ponies

Cornish Pasties

These animals aren't wild because they hold crazy parties! The ponies of Dartmoor (see p42) and Exmoor are wild in the sense that they are free to roam around the moor . . .

The ancient breeds found on Dartmoor and Exmoor are small and often dark coloured. They're also very tough – but then they have to be to survive the windswept moorland weather. Look out for their 'mealy' (meaning pale) noses.

No trip to Cornwall is complete without tasting a pasty. The oggy (as it's called in Cornish) is basically a semi-circular meat pie with a thick crust.

The pasty started life as lunch for tin miners (see p94). Workers would hold the crust with their grubby hands while scoffing the tasty filling. However, these days you're allowed to eat the whole thing! Head to The Lizard Pasty Shop (see p10) for particularly impressive pasties.

I SPOTTED:

- ☐ Wild Ponies
- ☐ Cornish Pasties
- ☐ Saint Piran's Flag
- ☐ High Hedgerows
- ☐ Clotted Cream

Saint Piran lived in the sixth century, nd was the patron aint of both Cornwall nd tin mining. His old, black-and-white ag has since become n emblem for the vhole county.

ook carefully as you travel round and you'll find e flag displayed in car nd shop windows. The ord Kernow (meaning Cornwall' in Cornish) is ften written on it. It's one ay that proud locals can ow off their roots!

Devon has more hedgerows than any other county in England - there are over 33,000 miles of them!

These ancient field boundaries support all kinds of wildlife. Some (like those around Dartmoor) are over 3,000 years old! You can tell their age by counting the number of species of woody bush in a thirty-metre stretch and multiplying that number by 100 years. So if you count seven different bush types, the hedge will be seven centuries old!

Clotted cream is popular in both Devon and Cornwall. It's a very dense type of cream that can be spread on snacks or dumped on desserts. **We think it's *cream-endous!***

We suggest you try it as part of a cream tea. Despite the name, this isn't tea with cream in it. Instead it's an awesome afternoon snack of scones, jam, clotted cream and tea. Or you could just stick a dollop of clotted cream on your pudding.

TOP FIVE

...beaches (Devon)

This region is famed for brilliant beaches - so grab a bucket and spade and get down to one of Devon's seaside spots!

I WENT TO:

- [ ] Saunton Sands
- [ ] Blackpool Sands
- [ ] Tunnels Beaches
- [ ] Barricane Beach
- [ ] Woolacombe Beach

Saunton Sands

Saunton Sands is a three-mile-long beach with impressive sand dunes and a posh hotel plonked in the middle.

It's superb for surfers and fantastic for families. Dogs are welcome and you'll find facilities including watersports equipment hire, a shop and a toilet. We suggest you combine a trip with a stop at Braunton Burrows, a nearby sand dune and nature reserve. It's got over 400 plant species - see how many you can count!

Saunton Sands
Braunton, EX33 1LQ

Blackpool Sands

Blackpool Sands is nowhere near th town of Blackpool a it isn't covered in sar But don't be put off the confusing name it's still a great beach

Blackpool Sands is a beautiful, crescent-shape beach surrounded by tree and covered in shingle (s pebbles). That makes it g for picnics, as you won't g sand in your sandwiches! You'll also find a sandpit, organic beach café, toilet showers and equipment f hire.

Blackpool Sands
Blackpool, Dartmouth, TQ6 (

Tunnels Beaches

Barricane Beach

Woolacombe Beach

Tunnels Beaches near Ilfracombe have a much less confusing name than Blackpool sands. That's because they're beaches full of, well, tunnels!

Access is via tunnels that have been carved into the rock. Then once you get to the beach you'll find a natural Victorian swimming pool that's filled (and emptied) by the tide. These are also some of the best rockpooling beaches in the UK, so don't forget your net, camera and jelly shoes.

Barricane might be small, but it's got a big reputation as a fantastic place to find shells.

Barricane is known to locals as Shell Beach because of the number of shells that wash up here. Over 40 types are regularly found on its shores! Look out for tiny cowrie shells, which come across the Atlantic from the Caribbean. See how many types of shell you can find and create a collage on the sand.

Woolacombe regularly wins awards as one of the best beaches in the UK. And with its three-mile long stretch of golden sand we can see why!

We like to go beachcombing here, then create a picture in the sand with the things we find. There are also great activities held on the beach during the summer. Look out for the National Sandcastle Competition in June, which attracts the best beach builders from all over England!

Tunnels Beaches
Bath Place, Ilfracombe, EX34 8AN

Barricane Beach
Between Woolacombe and Mortehoe, EX34

Woolacombe Beach
Woolacombe, EX34

TOP FIVE

...beaches (Cornwall)

Having listed some delightful Devon beaches, we thought we should also tell you about these cracking Cornish coves!

I WENT TO:

- [ ] Gwithian Beach
- [ ] Kynance Cove
- [ ] Polzeath
- [ ] Constantine Bay
- [ ] Pendower Beach

Gwithian Beach

Kynance Cove

This large, sandy beach near St Ives has a gentle slope and is ideal for running around.

Gwithian Beach is great for rockpooling – some of its pools are so large you can swim in them! It's also an ideal surfing spot, since the slope makes for slow-forming waves. The Gwithian Academy of Surfing is one of the best in Europe, so a session with them will set you up for surfing success!

We think Kynanc Cove on the Lizard (see p100) is o of the most beautifu beaches in the UK.

The sandy beach has steep cliffs on one side and a ver blue sea on the other. Heac there at low tide to explore shiny rock caves, which ha been worn down by the se Look out for serpentine roc – a multicoloured stone tha unique to the area. A cool also overlooks the beach.

Gwithian Beach
Gwithian, Hayle, TR27

Kynance Cove
Nr Helston, TR12 7PJ

Polzeath

Constantine Bay

Pendower Beach

Polzeath is one of the most popular beaches in Cornwall. Thankfully it's also big enough to have space for everyone no matter how busy it is!

The soft sand is great for playing beach games, building sandcastles and flying a kite, and the sea is brilliant for surfing. Why not try body boarding, or have a go on a kayak? There are also great coastal walks nearby if you want to abandon the sand.

Constantine is another classic Cornish beach. This sandy stretch is great for both bodyboarding and building things.

The bay lies on a popular piece of coast – the beaches of Harlyn, Treyarnon, Trevone and Booby's are all nearby. We suggest you head to the stream that runs down the middle of the beach and build a dam to divert the flow. Then why not walk to Booby's where you'll find great rocks for clambering over?

Pendower Beach is on Cornwall's south coast, not far from Truro.

It's covered by sand and shingle and is joined to Carne Beach, where you'll find remarkable rock pools. They're great for climbing across – just make sure you don't slip on the slimy seaweed! Look out also for seashells and mussels clinging to the rocks. Thankfully these tiny creatures don't mind sharing the beach – they might be shellfish but they're not selfish!

Polzeath
Nr Wadebridge, PL27

Constantine Bay
Nr Padstow, PL28

Pendower Beach
Roseland Peninsula, Nr Truro, TR2

TOP FIVE

...seaside towns

Well we do like to be beside the seaside . . . and these are our five favourite towns in the region where we can do just that!

Padstow

Salcombe

We suggest you bring your pocket money to Padstow (see p84), because it's got more fudge shops than we've ever seen in the same place!

We particularly like the Buttermilk Shop on Church Lane. Ask for a bag of their Cornish Tablet – it's a stupendous sugary treat! There's loads more to do here besides: you can admire the fishing boats in the harbour, chomp on fish and chips or try crabbing from the pier.

The best thing abo Salcombe is the boats. The shape of the sheltered estuary makes for a neat natural harbour – see how many boats you can count!

Salcome has a super sandy beach and a fun ferry whic runs between Salcombe ar South Sands. A sea tractor takes passengers between the boat and the South Sands beach. There's also a maritime museum and a whole host of walks along the coast.

I WENT TO:

- ☐ Padstow
- ☐ Salcombe
- ☐ Teignmouth
- ☐ Seaton
- ☐ Lynton and Lynmouth

Teignmouth

Seaton

Lynton and Lynmouth

Teignmouth is home to a brilliant beach and a proper pier. So head here for entertainment while perched above the waves!

Along the pier you'll find radio-controlled vehicles, video games, go-karts and other kids' rides. Then take a ride on the Teignmouth ferry, which connects the town with Shaldon Village. It's the oldest ferry in Britain and has been running for over 1,000 years! Look out for Shaldon's smuggler's tunnel, wihich leads to Ness Cove Beach.

Seaton is a pretty seaside town on Devon's Jurassic coast. As well as being home to a terrific tramway (see p20), this town also has a sloping shingle beach.

We suggest you take a walk along the seafront, then go pond dipping in Seaton Marshes Nature Reserve. The nearby Pecorama Model Railway is also well worth a visit – you can ride on mini-trains and admire the model railway exhibition.

Lynton is not technically a seaside town, as it's on top of a cliff! However, it is connected to Lynmouth and the seaside by a fantastic funicular (see p28).

Lynton and Lynmouth are two linked towns on the north Devon coast. The cliff road between them is so steep you feel like you might fall over the edge as you drive along! We love Lynmouth for its fantastic fish and chip shops and the dramatic Glen Lyn Gorge waterfall (see p29).

TOP FIVE

...walks

Devon and Cornwall both have beautiful scenery and wonderful wildlife. So put on some sensible shoes and take a walk on the wild side!

The South West Coast Path

We definitely don't suggest you try to walk this path in one go . . . because it's 630 miles long!

The South West Coast Path is like a hundred walks in one. It runs all the way along the Devon and Cornwall coast, beside spectacular seas and rugged cliffs, so there's bound to be a bit of it near you. Just watch your footing – some parts of it are narrow and can get quite slippery.

www.southwestcoastpath.com

Haldon Fores

Haldon Forest is n just home to an awesome aerial assau course – it's also a walking wonderland!

We suggest you walk or cycle along the forest's Discovery Trail. You'll find fun stuff along the way including a horizontal rope climbing frame – *Hald*-on tight as you clamber across it! The sensory trail also ha amazing views and things to touch along the way. Oh and there's a great café wit cracking cakes.

www.forestry.gov.uk

Decoy Country Park

Rachel Lambert's Wild Food Walks

Porlock Weir to Culbone

The word decoy means something misleading – but we're sure you won't feel tricked if you follow our advice and head to this country park!

Decoy Country Park contains a delightful lake surrounded by woodland and fields. You can hire rowing boats and canoes, then walk or cycle along one of the tracks. Look out for badger sets and see if you can spot woodland birds including buzzards, ravens, jays and woodpeckers.

Most of our recommended walks are based on a place, but this one's based on a person! Rachel Lambert will take you on a wild walk through nature . . .

Rachel's walks teach you about food which you can find in the wild. She provides recipes and tells stories along the way. We particularly like searching for seaweed! The walks run from different start points in Devon and Cornwall and usually take about two hours.

Moors are brilliant for windswept walks, and this trek across Exmoor is one of our favourites.

Start at Porlock Weir and take the coast path to Culbone, where you'll find tiny Culbone Church. At less than eleven metres long it's the smallest church in England and can't be reached by car! There's also a shed nearby where you can make yourself tea. Then either head back the way you came, or hike over Culbone Hill and complete the six mile round trip.

www.teignbridge.gov.uk

www.wildwalks-southwest.co.uk

www.westcountrywalks.com

TOP FIVE

...adventure playgrounds

Adventure playgrounds are like normal playgrounds, but with added activities and extra excitement! Here are five of our favourites.

I WENT TO:

- ☐ River Dart Country Park
- ☐ Colliford Lake Park
- ☐ Trevarno
- ☐ Lanhydrock
- ☐ Woodlands Theme Park

River Dart Country Park

This place is a very cool campsite, but day visitors are welcome to use the facilities too.

River Dart Country Park features a mind boggling range of activities. Scramble over nets, zoom down the zip wire or defend a pirate ship surrounded by water. And if that isn't enough, there are dramatic daredevil activities, such as water zorbs (inflatable floating balls which you stand inside), climbing and canoeing.

River Dart Country Park
Ashburton, Devon, TQ13 7NP
www.riverdart.co.uk

Colliford Lake Park

Colliford Lake Par▶ is home to the Ki Kingdom – a massive indoor and outdoor adventure playgroun◀

You'll be dazzled by drop slides, amazed by the net mazes and blown away by the ball pools. There are a' carts that you can race alon the woodland paths. Look out for deer as you drive! We particularly like the cra golf – but whatever activit▾ you choose at Colliford, y◀ definitely won't be bored!

Colliford Lake Park
St Neot, Cornwall, PL14 6PZ
www.collifordlakepark.◀

Trevarno

Lanhydrock

Woodlands Theme Park

Trevarno is a stunning stately home with grand gardens, but that's not why we're including it! We like it for it's wonderful woodland playground.

The play area is built to look like two castles, and they're packed with activities. You'll find swings, seesaws, slides, a climbing wall and a cargo net. There are even special climbing trees! There's Trevar-no way you'll want to miss it!

Trevarno
Crowntown, Nr Helston, Cornwall, TR13 0RU
www.trevarno.co.uk

Lanhydrock is another posh country house with an awesome adventure playground attached to it. And best of all, it's free to use!

The playground is in the woods behind the car park and contains slides, climbing nets, ropes and chin up bars. We particularly like the wobbly suspension bridge and the carved wooden animals which are dotted throughout the play area. You can also take a nature walk through the grounds from the car park.

Lanhydrock
Bodmin, Cornwall, PL30 5AD
www.nationaltrust.org.uk

Woodlands is a playground, zoo, farm, wildlife sanctuary and falcon centre all rolled into one!

The indoor playground has slides, scramble nets, ball blasting and a mirror maze. Outside, there's a commando course, aerial ninja towers and bumper boats. Or if you prefer you can admire the animals and see birds of prey in action in the falconry centre. It's a great day out in any weather.

Woodlands Theme Park
Dartmouth, Devon, TQ9 7DQ
www.woodlandspark.com

PARENTS' PAGE

Greetings, adult. This page is all for you. The rest of the book's for kids, so we thought it was only fair that you had your own page. So if you're a child, stop reading. Now. We said stop. Look, the whole rest of the book's for you. This is just for adults. There are tons more interesting things to do in the rest of the book – why not go to p10 and find out where you can drive a digger? In fact, we suggest you do anything but read this page. Stop reading right this second. Are you still there? No. Good.

So anyway, hello, adult.

Devon & Cornwall Unlocked is for children who are visiting places with adults. Very few of our sites admit unaccompanied children. So as you're likely to be the one planning the trip, we've included site details, such as telephone numbers and opening hours, on each page. Bear in mind that many sites are closed for the winter season, or only open selected weekends. Last admission is usually earlier than the closing time. We've also specified if there are height or age restrictions. While we have tried hard to ensure all the details are accurate at the time of going to press, things change, so it's best to check before you go anywhere.

Next: the Internet. We've tried to make sure that all the websites are child-friendly, but all the same, we suggest you supervise any surfing. We take no responsibility for third-party content and we recommend you check a site first if you are at all unsure.

Now for some general tips:

- Quite a few venues run good workshops and activities during weekends and school holidays. These are sometimes free, but may require advance booking.

- Many of the activities can be combined into a single day out. Use the maps at the beginning of each section to work out what things are near each other.

- Some of the activities in our book could be dangerous without appropriate adult supervision. Children using this book should be accompanied at all times.

- Many of the free activities in Devon and Cornwall involve walks or other locations, which don't have opening hours. We recommend you only go during daylight, and make sure you leave enough time to complete the walks.

Oh, and we think it's worth us mentioning that none of the sites in this book pay to be included.

Right then, that's the practical stuff out the way, and there's still a page to fill. So we've selected some facts about Devon & Cornwall just for grown ups. We don't think they're as interesting as the facts in the rest of the book, but then being an adult you don't really like interesting facts, do you now?

- Devon is the third largest English county by area. However it's only the eleventh largest county by population, with around 1.1 million people. Cornwall is almost half the size, and has a little over half a million inhabitants.

- Cornwall has its own nationalist movement, which is linked to the region's Celtic roots. Some people argue that Cornwall is in fact a territorial duchy, rather than a county of England. We're not sure what a territorial duchy is, so we don't know what to think.

- Cornwall has been marked on many maps as separate from England right up until the middle of the sixteenth century. Henry VIII listed England and Cornwall separately in the list of realms in his coronation address.

- Cornwall contains no actual walls made of corn, but it does have a few maize mazes.

- The world's first Jack Russell dog was bred by a Devonian priest called John Russell.

- Plymouth boasts the oldest commercial bakery in the world. F. H. Jacka opened in the sixteenth century, and baked biscuits for the Pilgrim Fathers.

- Tin mining began in Devon and Cornwall over 3,000 years ago. The Greeks used to call the area The Cassiterides, meaning The Tin Islands.

- In 1987 Belinda Carlisle released a chart topping single called 'Heaven Is A Place On Earth'. However, some people believe Belinda actually meant to say that 'Devon Is A Place On Earth' which is more factually accurate.

- Overland Clown is an anagram of 'Devon' and 'Cornwall'.

OK, that's your lot. Time to hand the book back to your child. Or, if you are a child who's read all of this, we hope you learned that stuff written for adults just isn't very funny.

INDEX

Here's an index of all the places included in the book, arranged in alphabetical order

INDEX

Where can you . . .

EAST DEVON

NORTH DEVON

SOUTH DEVON

CENTRAL CORNWALL

WEST CORNWALL

TOP FIVES

BACK-OF-THE-BOOK QUIZ

Good Luck!

The answers to all the following questions can be found somewhere in *Devon & Cornwall Unlocked*. Email a correct set of answers to us and you'll have a chance to win a signed and framed illustration of your choice from the book!

1 Who created the dancing diggers?

2 What is a pliosaur?

3 What is the world's largest freshwater fish?

4 How many stomachs do cows have?

5 How did the monkey puzzle tree get its name?

6 Why do camels have humps?

A. To store food
B. To store water
C. To store shoes

7 How many people rode the same surfboard in Australia in 2005?

A. 27
B. 37
C. 47

8 What is a bum roll?

A. A piece of bread shaped like a bum
B. An item of clothing that makes your bum look bigger
C. A stunt performed by special aeroplanes

9 If you were to go to a different Cornish beach each day, how long would it take you to visit them all?

A. Three and a half months
B. Five and a half months
C. Seven and a half months

10 Which of these things has not been used to make candles?

A. Sheep's fat
B. Beeswax
C. Cats' claws

Tie-breaker

In no more than 30 words, tell us what is your favourite place in the book and why.

Send your answers to **quiz@factfinderguides.co.uk**

Full terms and conditions are on our website.

ABOUT US

Joshua Perry and Emily Kerr

Emily and Josh went to school together. They highly recommend this as a starting point for anyone wanting to run a children's publishing company. Josh wanted to be a fireman and Emily hoped to be a Blue Peter presenter. Neither of them managed to achieve these goals, but they're OK with it now. Honest. Emily would like to go surfing all over Devon and Cornwall. Josh was born in Plymouth, and is an enthusiastic supporter of the Green Army.

Katherine Hardy (Kardy)

Kardy always wanted to have a pet pony. That would have been more feasible if she didn't live in central London. Quentin Blake has described her drawings as 'strong and subtly nuanced'. This is also not a bad description of her personality. She likes to take holidays in Harlyn Bay.

Allison Curtis

Allison was once part of a successful world record attempt to have the most people bouncing on space hoppers at the same time. Her cars are called Doris (the Morris) and Flossie (the Land Rover). Allison likes Devon and Cornwall so much she got married there, in Gwithian Church.

CREDITS

Authors: Emily Kerr, Joshua Perry
Series Editors: Joshua Perry, Emily Kerr
Design: Allison Curtis

Illustrations: Katherine Hardy
Maps: Allison Curtis, with reference to
OpenStreetMap – a free, editable map of the world

Thank yous ...

Cape Town for being a lot sunnier than London in winter. The wonderful Flickr photographers. Harlyn Farmhouse for being a brilliant base from which to research Cornwall. Claire, Alan, Maddy and Lottie for their hospitality and extensive knowledge of the Isles of Scilly. Izzy, Mark, Jack and Bailey for the chalet and general chat. Jean for love, laughter and lunacy. Harry and Matt for making our house move so smooth. Jack and Daisy for patiently waiting for their walkies while the book's design work was done. The escapethecity.org team for inviting us along. Hannah for demonstrating the ongoing diversity of a company secretary's role.

Photo Credits

11 Diggerland
13 flickr, Gavinandrewstewart
15 Mike Alsford
17 Phillip Brind
19 flickr, raeneff
21 Joe Ashworth
25 Nigel Lenton
27 Torrington1646
29 flickr, rightee
31 flickr, NickStenning
33 The Big Sheep
37 flickr, Didby Graham
39 NTPL/David Norton
41 Martin Brent Photography
43 flickr, me'nthedogs
45 flickr, kullez
47 flickr, Space & Light
49 flickr, Visentico/sento
51 National Maritime Aquarium
53 Paignton Zoo
55 Adrian Oakes
57 Dave Rowntree
59 Hazel Perry
63 flickr, jooliargh
65 flickr, tharrin
67 flickr, Kai Hendry

69 flickr, cloudsoup
71 flickr, ravels
73 Forrestry Commission
75 Eden Project
77 flickr, Andrew J. Kossman
79 flickr, ahisgett
81 flickr, fimb
83 flickr, law_kevin
85 Rick Stein's Seafood Restaurant
87 flickr, luckyfly
89 Alan Hingston
93 Bob Berry/NMM
95 flickr, Woodleywonderworks
97 Lynn Batton
99 flickr, a.froese
101 flickr, treehouse1977
103 Craig Hardman
105 NTPL/David Norton
107 Tate 2010
109 George Nixon
111 flickr, Nagillum
114 Flickr, me'nthedogs
114 Flickr, JoshuaHeller
115 Flickr, madnzany
115 Flickr, wwarby
115 Flickr, adactio

116 Flickr, roubicek
116 Flickr, Richard Barrett-Small
117 Flickr, agent_mikejohnson
117 Flickr, rightee
117 Flickr, Squidney
118 Flickr, Treehouse1977
118 Flickr, Benjgibbs
119 Flickr, Beatriz Rose Photography
119 Flickr, Steve Parker
119 Flickr, Heatheronhertravels
120 Flickr, Martin Pettitt
120 flickr, humbert15
121 Flickr, me'nthedogs
121 flickr, shirokazan
121 flickr, Sarah Elvin Photography
122 flickr, Tim Green aka atouch
122 Crown Copyright
123 Flickr, Brooke Anderson
123 Dan Thomas
123 flickr, me'nthedogs
124 flickr, hans s
124 flickr, Kevin Lawyer
125 Flickr, kwdesigns
125 Flickr, Edward Townend Photography
125 flickr, Gogoloopie